Your Body at Work

Also by David Givens, Ph.D.
Crime Signals
Love Signals

Your Body at Work

A Guide to Sight-reading the
Body Language of Business, Bosses,
and Boardrooms

David Givens, Ph.D.

ST. MARTIN'S GRIFFIN

NEW YORK

www.stmartins.com

Book design by level C

All illustrations by Aaron Huffman.

ISBN 978-0-312-57047-7

First Edition: September 2010

10 9 8 7 6 5 4 3 2 1

For my sons,
David Scott Givens and Aaron McKenna Huffman,
with love

Contents

Acknowledgments

I would like to thank my colleagues in anthropology, archaeology, biology, embryology, linguistics, neuroscience, psychiatry, psychology, and semiotics, who have studied human communication from a scientific point of view. I thank Yaniv Soha, my editor at St. Martin's Press, for his continued wisdom, grace, and guidance. Sincere thanks go to Eileen Cope, my agent at Trident Media Group in New York, for her support—and for making this project possible.

Foreword

When David Givens first approached me to write the foreword for this book I felt highly honored, considering who was asking. For nearly fifteen years I have been reading David Givens's work with considerable enthusiasm. To a great extent, he has formed and shaped my thinking on human behavior and nonverbal communications, which is reflected in my own writings. Those of us who have followed his work and used his dictionary on nonverbal communications will recognize him for what he is—a giant that lives among us.

David Givens writes as he teaches, as one would wish all professors taught, by opening the eyes of his students and then taking them on a journey of learning. It's an exquisite trip that adds clarity and nuance, and enriches our understanding of a world that communicates primarily nonverbally.

Unlike most writers, David Givens grants us access to how he thinks and sees the world, not just what he wants us to know. In doing so, he gives his work an anthropologist's perspective. He explores the *why* and *how* of humanity with a hint of impishness; for in many ways we behave, at times, no better than our nearest relatives—that is, the ones in the zoo. It is from that anthropologist's vantage point that he humbles us and, with a smile and a reverence for learning, makes us look deep inside at our primal behaviors so we can better understand ourselves. He puts up a mirror so we can see ourselves anew, with a fresh understanding of what it is to be human and how we communicate our thoughts and feelings.

In this, his latest work, he does not let us down.

Meticulously researched and utilizing all the sciences applicable (sociology, biology, neurology, psychology, anatomy, and physiology, to name a few), he shows us what drives our behavior and why we are influenced by such little things as how our hands look or where we choose to park our car. He examines body language in the workplace from head to toe, with the curiosity and inquisitiveness of a scientist who is yearning to find what others have missed. David Givens dissects the topic into the smallest of details: from what your hair says, to your eyes, to your hips, to your toes. What *Love Signals* did for dating and *Crime Signals* did for the study of crime, David Givens has now replicated for the business sector with this first-class work, *Your Body at Work*.

Replete with examples from today's business world, David Givens's new book explores the foundations of corporate behavior and communication. Only someone who has dedicated his life to understanding our species can talk about leadership, greed, trust, and deception in a corporate setting with David Givens's authority. What Desmond Morris did for the "naked ape," David Givens has now done for corporate apes: you and me.

If you love learning, if you love the sciences, if you love the why of human behavior, if you care about business communications, or if you are in human resources or management, then you will savor this book. This is a book that you can go back to over and over and find new nuggets of gold each time. It has a lot to teach us about ourselves.

Many books on nonverbal communications contribute to the literature, but every once in a while something comes along that sets a new standard and makes us stop and look with admiration.

I can count those books on one hand and, thanks to David Givens, I have one more to add to the list.

> —JOE NAVARRO, author of
>   *What Every Body Is Saying* and *Louder Than Words*
>   Tampa, Florida

The Body Politics
of Business

**That was one of the biggest moments of
my life, shaking that man's hand.**
—Sam Solovey, a contestant on Donald Trump's NBC-TV
series *The Apprentice* (O'Brien 2005, 22)

His body language is very outspoken. Protruding lips seem to point at you, and the comb-over hairdo has a name: "Taj Ma-helmet." To attract women, he once wore burgundy suits with matching patent leather shoes. Who is this man? He is self-reputed billionaire and deal-maker Donald John Trump, whose demeanor illustrates the power of body language in business, bosses, and boardrooms.

On the boardroom set of his reality TV show *The Apprentice*, as Donald Trump pointed with his right hand to say, "You're fired," you saw more than a simple gesture. As second-season *Apprentice* contestant Jennifer Crisafulli told the *Today* show, "There are little itty-bitty bullets that come flying, invisible bullets, out of his fingers into your chest" (O'Brien 2005, 22). To Ms. Crisafulli, Mr. Trump's gesticulation across the board table discharged a mysterious force through his fingertips. There was no doubt about it—when Trump said those words and pointed his hand, Jennifer felt the force and knew she was fired, for real.

The "invisible bullets" Ms. Crisafulli describes are meant to add emphasis—gestural firepower—to a boss's words. Trump-style hand movements are among thousands of nonverbal signs, signals, and cues that are sent and received each day in the workplace. They come regularly, nine to five, from co-workers, clients, managers, and bosses. Perhaps even more than written memos, text messages, and e-mail, nonverbal signs have the power to inspire or intimidate, to arouse sympathy, allegiance, anger, or fear.

We use the dramaturgy of Donald Trump's body language to begin a journey into the nonverbal world of work. En route we will explore uncharted dimensions of office space, decipher corporate messages encrypted in shoes, and watch expressive shoulders cajole in the boardroom. We will find hidden meaning in signals addressed to our senses of sight, touch, hearing, taste, and smell.

Let's start with smell. Consider the aroma of coffee, a seemingly commonplace beverage that in fact plays a major role in the workplace. In a February 14, 2007, memorandum to executives, Starbucks Chairman Howard Schultz lamented his company's switch from selling beans stored in open coffee bins to selling them packaged in flavor-locked bags.

"We achieved fresh-roasted bagged coffee, but at what cost?" he bemoaned. "The loss of aroma—perhaps the most powerful nonverbal signal we had in our stores" (Adamy 2007). As part of his job, Mr. Schultz visits thirty to forty Starbucks a week, and smell cues rank high on his agenda. At a Seattle-area store he complained about a strong odor of burnt cheese wafting from an oven-cooked sandwich. Since the cheesy smell detracted from Starbucks's aromatic coffee theme, Schultz had all of his outlets switch ovens. On the basis of scent, Schultz summarily "fired" the cookstove.

Donald Trump's hand gestures and Howard Schultz's aroma cues are just two of the workplace signals I've found. Workplace signals are the unspoken sights, sounds, textures, and scents that reveal what goes on in the work world apart from oral or written reports. The more you know about them, the better off you'll be in the nonverbal world of business, bosses, and boardrooms. With this book, I hope to give you a novel look at the sensory side of business that's completely off the organizational charts.

DAVID B. GIVENS, PH.D.
Center for Nonverbal Studies
Spokane, Washington

ONE

Bodytalk at Work

You can observe a lot by watching.
—Lawrence Peter ("Yogi") Berra

The workplace is a wordy place. Telephones, e-mails, keyboards, written reports, text messages, memos, and meetings. Hundreds, thousands, millions of words—printed, spoken, whispered, and shouted—greet you and compete for your undivided attention. Hear me, read me, heed me!

Your Body at Work, however, is not about words but about what lies beneath them: unspoken feelings, emotions, and moods. It's about what is left unstated—the hidden agendas, concealed plans, and covert schemes. There's often a secret motivation, program, or design beneath corporate verbiage. Sherlock Holmes wisely taught us to watch for hidden meaning in commonplace items like shoelaces, thumbnails, and sleeves. In *Your Body at Work* you will learn to decode and decipher hidden messages given off by nonverbal cues and body language in the workplace—from the crown of a head to the calcaneus of a heel. What do hands, shoulders, faces, and eyelids say in the boardroom that memos and words do not? How do business clothes make you look stronger or weaker, and more or less competent on the job? What secrets do corporate cupboards, cabinets, common areas, and cubicles hold?

There is meaning to be found everywhere in every office, in dress, décor, and demeanor.

In *Your Body at Work*'s subtitle, I introduce "sight-reading" to mean "intelligent observation." English "sight" comes from the seven-thousand-year-old Indo-European root word *sekw-*, "to perceive." Important senses of the English word "read" are "to anticipate through examination," and "to determine intent or mood" (Soukhanov 1992, 1504). Thus, sight-reading is the act of anticipating intentions and moods through the perceptive examination of nonverbal cues.

Learning to decode office signals will help you become not just a better listener but a better employee and supervisor. Watching body language as you listen will disclose the emotions behind words. Through active watching you will become more empathic, persuasive, and collaborative on the job. Moreover, seeing beneath spoken words will help you gauge the level of trust, or mistrust, among colleagues. Trust can be affirmed by acts as simple as a level gaze and denied by the subtle wink of an eye.

Perceptive listening, empathy, persuasion, collaboration, awareness, and trust are traits of a management style known as *servant leadership*. Servant leadership is the prescriptive notion that a boss should lead not just for the sake of amassing power but for the sake of employee well-being advanced toward a company's goals. Graduate students in my communication and leadership classes are often eager to apply servant leadership in their jobs. The goal is to lead less by edict than by example. By joining a last-minute envelope-stuffing session, for instance, a boss can show physical commitment to the project rather than simply dictating, "This mailing needs to get done right away."

As an anthropologist who specializes in nonverbal communication, I study how humans communicate apart from spoken, manually signed, and written words. After teaching for five years at the University of Washington in Seattle, I moved to the other

Washington, Washington, D.C. For twelve years there—in the city some have called the office capital of the world—I worked as an executive in association management. Upon returning to Washington State, I consulted professionally on matters of nonverbal communication for the U.S. Department of Defense, the Environmental Protection Agency, and the Federal Bureau of Investigation, and for corporations such as Masterfoods USA, Pfizer, Best Buy, Kimberly-Clark Worldwide, and Unilever. From fieldwork in diverse business habitats, I learned to decode the silent language of offices.

One of my favorite assignments was managing research for Unilever in the Language of Hands study. I knew that human hands had figured prominently in painting and sculpture, from ice age cave art to masterpieces by Michelangelo and Rodin, but I hadn't realized how critical hand messages could be in the boardroom. As colleagues discuss business face-to-face, they unconsciously monitor hands with a fine, albeit unconscious, eye.

What jumped out at me from the Unilever study was just how observant we are of each other's hands and their emotional signals. Like artists, we're acutely aware that wrists, palms, and digits have something important to say. Unlike artists, our own observations are often untutored, vague, and outside our conscious awareness. We get a feeling from a hand gesture, but can't easily put that feeling into words. Unlike Michelangelo, who studied human anatomy, most of us can't put a finger on the precise hand shape or position that made us notice that a mood shift had taken place. There's an intellectual disconnect between the gesture and the feeling.

To learn how ordinary people who are not artists decipher hands, my research team showed twelve high-resolution photographs of hand shapes and gestures to one hundred subjects in the greater Los Angeles, Kansas City (Missouri), Chicago, and Boston metropolitan areas. Photos ranged from the manicured hands of an education administrator to the rough-hewn hands of a working electrician. We asked, "What do these hands 'say' to you?" "What physical traits do you notice?" "What features do you like or dislike? Why?" "What hand would you least like to shake? Why?" And last, "What do you like best about your own hands? Why?" The nonrandom, nonprobability sample included 47 percent men and 53 percent women, aged eighteen to sixty-six (mean age was thirty-seven), whose occupations ranged from physician to donut cook.

We were amazed by the quality and quantity of the verbal responses. Subjects noticed a lot and had more than a little to say about hands, their shapes, sizes, conditions, and gestures. Without any prompting from my team of trained field anthropologists, respondents volunteered a total of 4,025 descriptors (words and phrases) to describe the twelve hand photos.

What did we learn about the silent language of business from the Unilever study? At a business meeting, the more unattractive a hand, the less likely a colleague will be to notice its gestures. In the study, as a hand's negative-appearance rating increased, the attention paid to its gestures and shapes decreased. Unsightly features competed for visual attention and simply got in the gesture's—and thus in the *gesturer's*—way. Participants were less able to read, interpret, and decode gestures made by the physically distressed hands. These were hands, again in the observers' own words, that showed "lines," "scars," "spots," "calluses," "dirt," "roughness," "dryness," "stains," "dry cuticles," and "ragged nails."

Conversely, the more attractive a hand, the more likely co-workers will notice and decode its signals. In the Language of Hands study we found that as a hand's positive-appearance rating increased, attention paid to its shape and gestures also increased. In short, participants were better able to see and decipher gestures produced by physically pleasant hands. Attractive hands were described as "clean," "groomed," "manicured," "cared for," "strong," "not dry," and "smooth."

Who knew there could be so much significance in something we often don't even know we're perceiving? Perhaps anthropologist Edward Sapir put it best when he wrote, "We respond to gestures with an extreme alertness and, one might almost say, in accordance with an elaborate and secret code that is written nowhere, known by none, and understood by all" (Sapir 1929, 137).

On July 25, 2002, the Language of Hands findings were shared at a press conference on the rooftop garden of the Library Hotel in New York City. "Working with the Center for Nonverbal Studies"—the private research organization I founded in 1997 in Spokane, Washington—"we better understand how people feel about their hands and the hands around them," said Unilever's hand-cream brand manager, Pablo Gazzera (White 2002).

Research from the University of Chicago shows that speaking gestures aid in verbal memory and enhance cognitive thought. Nonverbal hand cues thus augment the persuasive power of vocal words. They're key players in the silent language of business meetings, and your hands should be groomed for the parts they'll play above the boardroom table. But they're just one element in a whole language of nonverbal cues that you'll soon be introduced to.

DECIPHERING BODYTALK IN THE BOARDROOM

Think of a board meeting as you would a poker game. As poker guru and former FBI profiler Joe Navarro explains: "The major purpose of observation at the poker table is intelligence gathering—you want to learn as much as you can about each of your opponents at the table" (Navarro 2006, 10–11). At a card table or a conference table, the stakes are high, and in both games the player who watches body language has an edge.

From your swivel chair inside the boardroom, you watch as emotions flare above the tabletop. You see lips tighten, eyes roll, shoulders shrug, hands ball into fists. From these visible cues you're able to gauge—without words—where board members stand on issues. Like silent poker "tells," visible body movements tip hands.

As an anthropologist who studies body language, I'm some-times invited to sit in on private meetings held behind closed doors. "We'd like you to tell us," I'm asked, "what's really going on in our boardroom." So I enter as a guest, sit quietly, and fold my arms on the table. I mentally turn down the sound so the room's constant chatter won't break my concentration. I want to observe how meeting-goers behave rather than hear what they say. Known as "unobtrusive observation," this is the method used by Jane Goodall to study wild chimpanzees in Africa. To better observe the chimps' body movements and gestures, Goodall would momentarily ignore their distracting pant-hoots, waa-barks, and vocal screams. What the apes did in the rain forest often mat-tered more than what their voices said.

In the boardroom, I'd watch human hands, arms, and shoul-ders flex, extend, pivot, and dance above a conference table's per-fectly level playing field. In my role as visiting anthropologist, I imagined the tabletop the way Goodall might have seen East Africa's Serengeti Plain. I pictured lions, jackals, and wildebeests competing for survival of the fittest. On the corporate flatland's polished surface, colleagues shuffled papers, dueled with hand gestures, and conducted business face-to-face. Depending on the agenda item discussed, they gave each other pensive, quizzical, sheepish, or dogged eye contact. That each person would speak— loudly or softly, some more often than others—was the norm. Busi-ness meetings are nothing if not verbal. But what did lips, eyes, and fingertips say that words did not? What was the meeting's unspoken agenda, its unwritten subtext? My job was to make sense of the drama by assessing bodytalk.

The Case of the Missing Gesture

A curious facet of bodytalk is that feelings, opinions, and moods may be expressed with or without movement. A hand that slaps a table, for instance, may show insistence or anger, while a hand that hides beneath the tabletop can show disengagement or withdrawal from the group. There is meaning, whether or not the hand actually moves.

I observed a telling case of "silent hands" at a twenty-minute meeting I videotaped in Seattle, Washington, in the early 1980s. The 1980s saw ever-increasing numbers of women entering the workforce, many finding themselves for the first time in serious, head-to-head competition with men. Barbara, one of the meeting participants, spent the entire time with both hands held in her lap under the table. Though she spoke up on issues, her hands remained invisble with nothing at all to say. From the videotape it was clear that Barbara's six male colleagues paid very little attention to either her or her comments. They looked at each other but seldom even glanced Barbara's way.

As I replayed the video for her, Barbara's hand gestures seemed even more conspicuous by their absence. By not engaging others with her hands as she listened or spoke, Barbara's demeanor suggested little interest in the meeting. More important, her behavior showed little concern for participants in the room. She seemed as unmoved by the meeting's agenda as she was removed from the group. To human eyes, what cannot be seen appears not to exist, and Barbara had, without intention or awareness, turned herself into a nonentity.

When Barbara and I reviewed the meeting tape, Barbara told

me she'd felt that none of her remarks were taken seriously by her colleagues. This contributed to her posture of disengagement—leaning backward in her chair, angling her upper body away from speakers (instead of orienting to them), and keeping her hands perfectly still. Since my role was advisory to the Seattle group, I recommended that in future meetings Barbara place both hands on the tabletop and reach out with them—gesture—to bring others into her personal space and sphere of influence. Since body movements attract eyes, moving a hand is enough to bring notice. It's like waving to attract someone's attention across a room: "Hey, look, I'm over here!"

Reaching an open hand across a board table adds immediacy by addressing comments to colleagues directly. The gesture proffers an unwritten invitation to connect. Adding personality and movement to spoken words makes them seem more personal and attention-worthy. While words themselves address the left-brain's speech centers (such as Wernicke's area), gestures appeal to emotional areas of the right-brain hemisphere. Expressing emotion with gestures as you speak thus addresses both sides of a listener's brain at once. This makes for a palpably stronger statement and testifies to your own firm belief in what you have to say. Hand gestures not only accent but stand behind words to validate them.

Moreover, hand movements reduce the physical distance separating you from listeners. Colleagues feel closer as you literally and figuratively reach hands out toward them. Their primate-inspired brains interpret your reaching as an implicit intention to reach out and touch. Above a boardroom table, an extended, opened palm emits the same positive message one sees and feels in a handshake's preparatory reach. The reaching movement itself sends a powerful message of affiliation.

In chapter 4 we'll thoroughly decipher the meaning of hand shapes and gestures in the workplace. But already, from Barbara's case, we've seen how critical hands can be in a business meeting.

They are certainly an important player in our nonverbal language at work—though they're far from the only one.

Getting a Hand-on-Hip

Former game warden Jeff Baile's workplace was once the great outdoors of Peoria County, Illinois. As a law officer employed by the Illinois Conservation Police, Baile held countless ad hoc meetings in the field with total strangers, men who worked in the illegal business of poaching. A student of body language, Baile would warily approach strangers in the bush and use sight-reading to assess their moods and intentions before meeting them face-to-face. One of Jeff's most trusted body-language cues was what I call *hands-on-hips,* also known as *arms akimbo* (Morris 1994, 4).

"I've always been fascinated with the arms akimbo gesture," Jeff wrote in an e-mail, "and use it all the time while on patrol. I've found that, in situational context, it usually means the person is in a negative state of mind. Thus, if an officer can see this, it's a heads-up there may be trouble. And I've even caught myself doing it when I'm upset. I've found it quite reliable in determining state of mind, which is important for any law enforcement officer" (Baile 2000b, personal comm.).

Hands-on-hips is a worldwide gesture in which the palms rest on the hips, with the elbows flexed outward and angled sharply away from the body. As with words, hands-on-hips may have several meanings, but the most common one, as Jeff Baile notes, is that a person is in a defensive or negative frame of mind. Most often used while standing, I've also seen a distinctive one-armed version of the akimbo gesture given in staff meetings, from the seated position, when negative emotions and resistance run high.

One hand-on-hip case in particular stays etched in my memory. It was given by a large, heavyset, middle-aged man I'll call "Dan." Dan's flexed right arm had locked onto his right hip as he sat

*Hand-on-hip can signal
an aggressive state of mind.*

listening to "Liz," a young woman half his size with whom he
sharply disagreed. His imposing upper body leaned forward over
the meeting table, and angled toward Liz on the other side with
his shoulders aimed squarely at her. Dan's lips tensed and parted
as he stared across the table into Liz's face. His out-flung right
elbow was in prominent view for all in the room to see. Like a
cobra spreading its hood, Dan seemed poised to strike. His hand-
on-hip clearly signaled an aggressive state of mind.

As Jeff Baile writes in "'Bowing Out' Means Trouble," an article for *International Game Warden,* "It's pretty hard to tell how people
may feel about us as we approach them in the field. Is this going to
be a run-of-the-mill check with no problems—or a confrontation?
There is a [hands-on-hips] gesture that people make, though,
that helps answer this question. It's produced unconsciously
when people are irritated about something and it can be seen from
yards away if you're paying attention" (Baile 2000a, 8). From just
a few feet away, since all eyes were turned on Dan, his co-worker
Liz and everyone around the conference table must have been

aware of the man's polemic mood. Dan's hand-on-hip clearly registered his negative stance for all to see.

My colleague in nonverbal studies, Joe Navarro, then a special agent with the FBI, sent me an e-mail that agreed with Baile's interpretation of hands-on-hips, seen so vividly in the example of Liz and Dan above: "In my experience, it is a territorial-claiming gesture usually present when something is wrong. Many a child has come home to a mother waiting at the door with her arms akimbo. Nothing further need be said: The kid is in trouble" (Navarro 2001, personal comm.).

In the field, in meetings, or in the home, seeing hands-on-hips is an indication of annoyance, disagreement, or anger. Studies show that we use arms akimbo more with people we dislike than with those we like. According to biologist Desmond Morris, hands-on-hips is a worldwide gesture that often means "keep away from me. This is an unconscious action we perform when we feel antisocial in a social setting. It is observed when sportsmen have just lost a vital point, game or contest" (Morris 1994, 4).

Though often a negative sign, in the workplace hands-on-hips can also have positive connotations. As a manager explains a new work project to an employee, for instance, the latter's akimbo stance can show that his or her body has prepared to take steps to perform, take part in, or take charge of the event, activity, or assignment. In this context, hands-on-hips discloses that an employee's body has synched into "ready mode," poised to step forward and carry out the superior's task; the akimbo cue suggests a positive, eager attitude akin to rolling up sleeves to get the job done.

A Case of Pursed Lips

Thus far, we've seen a few things our hands can say—or fail to say—in the workplace. Hands are indeed our "great communicators," and we'll take an in-depth look at more of their gestures and

The human face practically bristles with cues.

emotional meanings in chapter 4. But as we'll see, another prime anatomical area for sight-reading in the workplace is the face. A human face practically bristles with cues.

One of the more telling cues to look for while sight-reading your boss's face at a meeting is the *lip purse* (you'll learn a great deal more about lip cues in chapter 2). As an informant for *Your Body at Work,* Dave told me, "I can always tell what my boss is thinking about my ideas at our Monday meetings by something funny he does with his lips. He starts making these little lip movements like he's sucking out of a straw." Dave added, "When he starts doing this I know he'll have some issue or problems with my idea. So when I see it I sort of back up and rephrase what I'm saying to get that look off his face before I go on. When he's not doing the lip thing I know I'm okay."

The "lip thing" Dave sees is an acute burst of lip-pursing movements on his boss's face. In pursing, you will see the lips repeatedly evert (rotate outwards), pucker, and round in a look of disagreement, scheming, or calculated thought. The lip purse's paramount message is a thoughtful dissentience that says, "I disagree." The tightly screwed-out lips of the purse cue, which some liken to a pig snout, show that a listener has gone beyond the ordinary pout of uncertainty to a palpably negative, dissenting frame of mind.

As a mood sign, the lip purse Dave sees reflects an alternative verbal reply taking shape in his boss's brain. The shaping happens in the primary speech center known as Broca's area, a finger-size patch of neocortex involved in the production of spoken words. In the act of pursing, the lips' *orbicularis oris* muscle contracts. This muscle is a sphincter consisting of (1) *marginal* muscles, located beneath the visible margin of the lips themselves; and (2) *peripheral* muscles, located around the lips' periphery from the nostril bulbs to the chin. In human beings the lips' marginal muscles (*pars marginalis*) are uniquely developed specifically for speech.

In Dave's boss, pursed lips signal resistance to what he feels are unattractive ideas raised at staff meetings. The purse signifies that an alternative idea or objection has formed in Broca's area of the boss's brain. In the brain of our closest living animal relative, the chimpanzee, a motor area analogous to Broca's controls the rounded, pursed-lip movements chimps use to make facial grimaces and emotional calls (Lieberman 1991). The pant-hoot cry of excitement mentioned earlier in relation to Jane Goodall's chimps is a case in point. The boss's rounded, pursed-lip movements are neither as visible nor as emotional as pant-hoots, but still point to a noticeable shift in state of mind. You can see quarrelsome words forming before they come out through the lips.

SIGHT-READING AFTER THE MEETING

**When Roberts was mad his lips became
small and tight, slits on an angry face.**
—Portrait of KKR partner George Roberts on the day RJR
Nabisco fell (Burrough and Helyar 1990, 481)

In the workplace, face-to-face board meetings, client meetings, and staff meetings are all fertile grounds for sight-reading. But what if you're an outsider not invited to the meeting? You can still monitor body language from a strategic vantage point—for instance, between the boardroom and nearest restroom. Caffeine is a mild diuretic, so coffee in the boardroom guarantees that board members will come out. As they walk the hallways, the tightened lips, balled fists, and slumped shoulders displayed inside will become visible outside: Since emotionally responsive muscles of the face, shoulders, and hands let go of feelings slowly, fear, uncertainty, and anger will continue to show, even as they've left the boardroom behind them. As if obeying Newton's first law, emotions set in motion tend to linger.

In 1989, during one of the biggest leveraged buyouts in U.S. history, restroom surveillance paid off handsomely for KKR (Kohlberg Kravis Roberts & Co.) when it purchased RJR Nabisco. To monitor RJR's board meeting, which was held behind closed double doors, KKR craftily chose a nearby vacant office, located some twenty feet away from the conference room, in which to wait out the decision on their $25 billion takeover bid.

As coffee filled corporate bladders, RJR board members walked past KKR associates who'd been assigned to "urinal patrol" (Burrough and Helyar 1990, 488). KKR associates went on restroom walkabout to watch for telling signs—depleted groans; strained smiles; discernible shrugs, winks, and nods—to learn where RJR's board stood on the bidding. "Going to the bathroom," one board member reported, "was like facing a receiving line" (Burrough and Helyar 1990, 492).

KKR's chief rival in the game to acquire RJR Nabisco was the latter's own CEO, F. Ross Johnson. Unlike KKR's principal player, Henry Kravis, Ross Johnson elected to wait out RJR's decision at a distance in an office removed from the action, three floors below the boardroom. Being so far away, Johnson and his colleagues failed to pick up on the bodytalk and emotional chatter upstairs.

Had Ross Johnson only seen the anxious faces, knowing looks, conspiratorial smiles, and angry outbursts displayed in the hallway above, he might have realized his board was seriously torn between the two bidding rivals. The demeanor outside the meeting room disclosed what was later acknowledged to be a virtual tie between members who favored Johnson and those who favored KKR. The board's vote, in other words, could well have gone either way.

Sensing a tie from the board's body language, KKR tried harder. Neither seeing nor sensing the tie, Ross Johnson stood pat. Had he read the available bodytalk and showed up at the board meeting to plead his case, he might have won. But rather, staying a figurative arm's length away downstairs while KKR watched from upstairs, Mr. Johnson lost the bidding war. At the final hour, a board member officially moved to award RJR Nabisco to KKR, and the move was seconded. "All in favor," said the board's chairman. As Bryan Burrough and John Helyas write in *Barbarians at the Gate,* "Hands filled the air. 'All opposed?' No hands" (Burrough and Helyar 1990, 499).

From my own perspective as an anthropologist who studies nonverbal communication, I'd bet on players who take time to read gestures, signs, and body-language cues. As Phil Hellmuth, Jr., winner of eleven World Series of Poker bracelets, wisely notes, you can either learn to read body language or become an open book that others read.

In *Your Body at Work,* you will learn to read the body language of co-workers, colleagues, board members, and bosses. Seemingly minor palm shrugs, tensed lips, and sidelong glances can reveal opinions and moods not disclosed in memos or e-mail. You will also learn to decipher nonverbal signs of the workplace setting itself, from costly artwork on corporate walls to the whimsical smiley face on a cubicle divider. Each has a revealing tale to tell.

Recall the major purpose of observation: intelligence gathering. You want to learn as much as you can about your boss, the people you work with, and the mysterious habitat known as the office.

In the next chapter, you will learn to decode the faces you see each day at work. A person's visual trademark, the face defines corporate identity, expresses unspoken moods and opinions, and shows how we relate to others on the job. You may not tell a colleague, in so many words, precisely what you feel—but a noticeably dimpled chin tells all.

———

Face Value

Get that look off your face!
—Mom (your first and dearest boss)

The face is every human's visual trademark and our species' most photographed body part. For 99.99 percent of our existence as *Homo* we watched other faces, but rarely saw our own except as glimpsed in ponds and pools. Capturing a face in pictures or mirrors has been likened to capturing the soul. That in so many societies the face is said to reflect the soul bespeaks the nonverbal power of its landmarks.

Nowhere is a businessperson's facial power more graphically depicted than in *The Wall Street Journal.* On its pages, stippled portraits called hedcuts distill the essence of business faces into tightly cropped head-and-shoulders sketches designed to showcase hair, eyes, and facial features with bristling dots and crosshatched lines.

Introduced to the *Journal* by artist Kevin Sprouls in 1979, the pen-and-ink hedcuts usually show serious faces in repose, with minimal animation of features. In the March 22, 2007, hedcut of Borders CEO George Jones, for example, Mr. Jones peers at us through calm eyes from a seemingly disembodied face. His short business hair, pressed suit, and knotted tie hardly seem to matter next to his tranquil gaze. In the October 29, 2008, hedcut of

Donald Trump, Mr. Trump's hair threatens to crash upon his serious brow like a wave from the Banzai Pipeline. The swelling hair is all that seems to matter.

Hedcuts accent facial strengths and weaknesses. They reveal the sharpest of contrasts, for instance, between Donald Trump's "power face" and the boyish mien of Microsoft's former boss William H. Gates III. If Mr. Trump's face is basically rectangular, broad across the cheekbones, and wide across the lower jaw, Mr. Gates's oval face is narrow, with a slender lower jaw that exhibits some disharmony between its skeletal support and soft tissues. Bill Gates's lower face is more spheroid than squared-off.

Trump wears a more dominant, and Gates a more submissive, business face. What do dominant faces look like? According to Syracuse University sociologist Allan Mazur: "Faces identified as dominant are more likely to be handsome—to be muscular, to have prominent as opposed to weak chins, and to have heavy brow ridges with deep-set eyes. Submissive faces are often round or narrow" (Mazur and Keating 1984, 134). Dr. Mazur has found that facial dominance correlates well with higher achieved rank in the U.S. military. In the marines, a Donald face trumps the weaker face of a Bill Gates.

The look of your face in business or battle is undoubtedly important, but how you animate its features is more important still. Facial animation—the mobility of your chin, lips, tongue, cheeks, eyelids, and eyebrows—is the focus of this chapter. If Bill Gates shows a mischievous grin, The Donald shows a pugnacious pout. Which face would you rather do business with? What unintended messages do you convey with *lip purses, lip pouts,* and in-rolled *lip compressions*? How would you decipher a boss's chronic look of astonishment, discomfort, or disbelief? When is biting the lip more likely than smiling to settle an argument? We'll answer these questions and more as we circumnavigate the facial plain, learning to read—and make—faces for success and profit in the workplace.

THE SMILE

Smiley Faces

A whimsical fixture in many offices today is the yellow smiley face. It beams pure joy from posters, stickers, office doors, bulletin boards, and bouncy balls. Since smiles are contagious, seeing a smiley face can put you in a happier mood. Smiley seems to say, "This is how our office should feel, all day!" The reality, of course, is that most colleagues are too busy to feel happy, while some, judging from droopy faces, feel grumpy, sad, or depressed. I've observed more smiley-face decorations in cubicles than in corner offices with views.

The smiley face was designed by commercial artist Harvey Ball in the 1960s (Honan 2001). Since then it has become a universal graphic symbol of happiness. Its yellow hue is associated with the sun's cheering brightness. The round face, paired eye-spots, and curvilinear smile are instantly recognizable in any culture, from New Guinea to New York. Mr. Ball designed the happy face schema to enhance his Worcester, Massachusetts, State Mutual Life Assurance Company's "friendship campaign" to bolster employee morale. It reportedly took Mr. Ball just ten minutes to complete the design. (Missing in his first sketch, Ball added eye spots so disgruntled employees wouldn't be tempted to turn the smile upside down to show a frown.)

According to son Charlie Ball, Harvey "understood the power of [the smiley face] and was enormously proud of it [even though others, not Ball, profited financially from the design]. He left this world with no apologies and no regrets, happy to have this as his legacy" (Woo 2001, A6).

A second smiley-face office icon was born on September 19, 1982, at Carnegie Mellon University in Pittsburgh, Pennsylvania. Its inventor, Scott E. Fahlman, posted the following note in ASCII to the school's computer science bulletin board: "I propose that the following character sequence [be used] for joke markers: :-)." The semantics of Mr. Fahlman's joke marker evolved into cuter versions of today's smile, such as the ☺. You can add a sliver of happiness to the driest e-mail by adding :-) after "Thank you."

Scott Fahlman's joke marker was an "emoticon" (emote= "emotion," icon="picture"). Since e-mailed words aren't softened by friendly shoulder shrugs, winks, or smiles, they may seem brusque or insistent. We now have hundreds of computer images to choose from to add positive sentiments to bolster rapport. Many emoticons are modified versions of Mr. Fahlman's original symbol, such as ;) for "wink," XD for "laughing hard," and :] for "smirk." That our writing system, which evolved from ancient picture writing, is once again using pictographs gives testimony to the power of emotion, even in digital messages and texts.

The Courtship Smile

A smile may have many meanings in the office. For one who's attracted to you, your own smile's come-hither message can say, "I'm attracted to you, too." In countries like Italy, Mexico, and Nigeria, a woman who smiles at a man is seen as giving an open invitation to approach. In overseas assignments, American businesswomen should be wary of the unintended effects of gratuitous grinning.

In the late 1990s a hybrid grin known as the "supermarket mandatory smile" originated in the United States. Safeway, Inc., the second-largest supermarket chain in the United States, instructed its employees to smile and greet customers with direct eye contact.

In 1998 an article in *USA Today*, "Safeway's Mandatory Smiles Pose Danger, Workers Say," reported that twelve female employees had filed grievances over the chain's smile-and-eye-contact policy, after numerous male customers reportedly propositioned them for dates.

Soon after, however, Safeway rescinded its mandatory smile-policy initiative. In the workplace, women should always be aware that an innocent, friendly smile can trigger unwanted attention from attracted male colleagues. Adding a coy head tilt or lifting your shoulders submissively as you smile will make the attraction even stronger.

The Smile Is Your Costume

I borrowed this title from Japanese artist Momoyo Torimitsu, who used the words in her art exposition—"Smile :-), Wear It Like a Costume!"—presented at the 2008 International Symposium on Electronic Art (ISEA) in Singapore. Ms. Torimitsu had collected a photo gallery of smiles from Singapore residents, and displayed them to show the variety of messages that smiles convey among people from diverse professions, from corporate executives to exotic dancing. "The smile," she says, "is probably the most powerful expression we have in our repertoire of facial gestures." From years of watching body language, I wholeheartedly agree.

Momoyo Torimitsu achieved artistic fame earlier in 1996 in New York City when she exhibited a life-size robotic puppet on the sidewalks of Broadway. The puppet—part of her performance exhibit titled "Miyata-san in Action"—was designed to look like a suited-up Japanese executive or "salary man." Dressed in a white nurse's uniform, Ms. Torimitsu walked beside the puppet and assisted Miyata-san as he crawled on his elbows and knees, military style, down sidewalks, forging ahead through imagined corporate firepower to do business and achieve success at any cost. Instead of smiling, the bespectacled Mr. Miyata had what looked like seriously tensed lips and a rigid, determined face fit for combat.

After collecting her gallery of Singaporean smiles, Ms. Torimitsu concluded that different professions each have their own particular brands of smile face, which she likens to corporate uniforms or costumes. Her artistic exhibit in 2008 sought to explore, in her words, "the subtle messages of compliance, attraction, persuasion, and power that the smile sends out, and how our society interprets them."

Descended from the primate "fear grin," the human smile is a universal gesture given throughout life, from infancy until death. The "polite smile"—showing only the top teeth—plays an important supporting role in the job interview. In monkeys and apes, the fear grin shows a feeling of deference or timidity to telegraph a lack of aggressiveness. In human beings the deferential smile we show the boss is a functional fear grin. We feel a bit cowed and it shows. Yet our smile evolved beyond the fear grin, adding many subtle and emotional overtones.

The grin on your receptionist's face as she phones her new boyfriend is an expression not of deference but of joy. As Momoyo Torimitsu points out in her exhibit, the smile can range from jubilance to politeness to sadism. Picture the grin Oddjob gave James Bond in *Goldfinger* (1964) as the sadistic chauffeur crushed a golf ball in his palm to threaten 007 with a show of strength. Should your boss give an Oddjob smile as he transfers you to the Barstow office, it may be time to update your résumé.

In photos taken at the 2008 ISEA in Singapore, Ms. Torimitsu wears what psychologists call a "true smile." Not only do her lips curve upward into a grin, but the outer corners of her eyes crinkle to the point of eyelid closure. Had she given an intentional "camera smile" instead, you would see only the grin. There would be no involvement of the muscles around her eyes. Given on demand, the more calculated, less emotional camera smile can be patronizing. Given by vendors, it's a sign they'd like to sell you more toner than the office needs.

Seeing a smile on a colleague's face is one of the rewards of working face-to-face in an office. The happy feeling it conveys is contagious. When a colleague smiles at you in the elevator, you sense her gladness is real. Your eyes see the smile face and your optic nerves send its uplifting message to a region of the occipital lobe, located at the very rear of your brain. Mirror neurons there and in the brain's emotional centers fire off to make you feel the glad emotion beaming from your coworker's face. Your brain mirrors your colleague's brain; you return the message in kind and walk it down the hallway for others to see. Whether the signal arises from an associate's face or a smiley face on a door, the response is usually the same: a mild or moderate feeling of joy.

YOUR EMOTIONS

Don't Let Them See You Cry

Like the stock market, feelings are volatile and liable to sudden changes. In the office emotions can change on a dime. One minute you're up, and then, after an unfriendly e-mail or disappointing phone call, you are down. The first sign of a cry coming on is a quivering of the chin. The *mentalis,* the small muscle that contracts to cause the skin's quiver, is shown by electromyography (EMG) studies to be one of the most emotional muscles in the human body. Thus, when a cry starts it's almost impossible, short of growing a beard, to keep the quiver and dimpled skin from showing.

The second sign of crying, equally hard to control, is the visible outflow of moisture—tears—from the eyes' lacrimal glands. The musclelike organs that contract to expel teardrops are also under emotional control; once they contract, it's hard to stop the flow.

Since a woman's tear glands produce more moisture than a man's, her cry face is harder to mask and easier for everyone around the table to see.

The third sign of crying is gross puckering of all the facial muscles as the face collapses into a full-fledged sob. The all-too-visible puckered-face cry reveals a person who's emotionally depleted and out of control. Showing colleagues you are out of control is the principle problem with crying in the office.

In January 2008 U.S. senator Hillary Clinton showed the first two signs of a cry as she campaigned in Portsmouth, New Hampshire, for the office of U.S. president. The moment was captured on TV and commented on by political pundits around the country. In an interview with Helena Andrews of Politico. com, who asked if Senator Clinton was faking the cry, I noted that the pained facial expression and catch in the throat seemed genuine. "I really doubt she could have scripted it or planned for it," I said (Andrews 2008).

Hillary Clinton's cry face got mixed reviews from the public. Many praised her for sharing an emotional moment on the campaign trail. Others accused her of crocodile tears, of faking the cry to bewail unfair treatment she'd received from rivals (men) in the primary campaign. Most of the people I talked to thought Senator Clinton's watershed, though spontaneous, was an unfortunate show of weakness.

"Crying at work isn't something any woman wants to do, especially in front of men, who too often view tears as a sign of weakness and reinforcement of stereotypes that women are 'too emotional,'" writes Lorna Collier in her *Chicago Tribune* article, "When a Good Cry Just Doesn't Work" (Collier 2004). Ms. Collier cites the case of Alexandra Levit, a young woman who cried twice in front of her boss at a high-pressure public relations office in New York City. Ms. Levit's weeping episodes cost her a promotion, which led to her quitting the firm (Collier 2004). "I can't take it when they cry," a Fortune 500 company male executive wrote about women colleagues who publicly weep on the job. "I want to shake them or hug them, but you can't really do either" (Bing 2004).

When you feel a cry coming on, substitute anger instead. Adopt a fighting mood to counteract the cry's surrender to flight. Visualize yourself punching the boss in the stomach or nose. In the office anger is a more productive emotion to show than defeat.

Emotional Networking

On November 24, 2008, the following want ad ran on Craigslist:

> Hi,
> If you live within 20 minutes of Westport and are a happy, people person who likes to stay busy, please apply. This job is M–F, 9–3, in an extremely busy office. Please have great computer and phone skills. (Anonymous 2008c)

We've seen that smiles and happy feelings in the office are contagious. How contagious was revealed in landmark research on 4,739 people whose happiness was tracked over a twenty-year period from 1983 to 2003 (Fowler and Christakis 2008). The study found that one person's happiness can positively affect another's for up to a year (B. Stein 2008, A12). The researchers learned that happiness comes not from raises, promotions, or winning the lottery, but simply from being around others who are happy.

Like catching the flu from a co-worker, you can also catch happiness. Moreover, you can infect colleagues, who in turn infect spouses, who then infect their friends with the happiness bug. The longitudinal social-network study by Nicholas Christakis of Harvard University and James Fowler of the University of California, San Diego, used data from the legendary Framingham

Heart Study. As Dr. Fowler said in an interview, "[Our] work shows that whether a friend's friend is happy has more influence than a $5,000 raise" (B. Stein 2008, A12).

For happy people, the glad emotion is obtained and reinforced through contact with other happy people in overlapping social networks. Those in the network whom you may never even see— for example, friends of your co-worker's friends—have an influence as well. In the office, the study suggests, happiness may span up to three degrees of separation.

Happiness is a visceral feeling of contentment, well-being, or joy brought on by stimulation of pleasure centers of the brain. Nonverbally, happiness may show in smiles, laughter, and eyebrow flashes of recognition. The eyebrow flash is a universal human signal given, for instance, when a receptionist greets you with a quick lifting of both eyebrows. Happiness, which shows most clearly in the lower face and eye area, first becomes visible in babies between five and seven months of age.

In the office, happiness can be apparent on the first day of work. Such is the intention, at least, of the want ad on the previous page. The company may not have read the latest research, but someone was savvy enough to want to fill a social-networking node with a happy employee. Return on investment on such a decision would likely be immediate and last for years.

Face Crumple

Facial expressions are contagious, especially for children. When a child sees happiness in a parent's face, he or she shows a happy face back. Seeing sadness scripts a child, conversely, to feel sad. When life in the office becomes stressful, children sense the parent's negative emotion and feel stressed themselves.

When three-year-old Bailey Haag of Tonawanda, New York, heard fearful tones in her mother's voice as she spoke to Bailey's dad about his job layoff, emotion showed on her face. "The little girl's brow furrowed and her face grew sad as she overheard her mother on the phone reacting to . . . her father's layoff," reporter Sue Shellenbarger wrote in *The Wall Street Journal* (Shellenbarger 2008, D1). Claire Haag, Bailey's mother, said, "It was not a good conversation," and noticed her daughter's face crumple.

Reading the crumpled face as a sign of distress, Ms. Haag quickly came up with a plan. She told Bailey to give her daddy "lots of hugs when he [came] home." When disturbing office events make their way into the home, as they invariably do, parents need to shield their children with extra care. By giving her little girl a way to express positive emotions, Ms. Haag did the right thing.

———

In this chapter we've read the face as a signboard of emotions, feelings, and moods. Since feelings are often deliberately unstated on the job, we look to the face rather than to words for answers. The more you know about the face's principle landmarks and their movements, the better you will be able to see inside your colleagues' heads. In the next chapter, you will learn to read what your colleagues say with their most expressive facial feature.

THREE

Seeing Eye to Eye

As soon as I walked into the room, that man looked
at me, immediately looked away, and never met
my eyes during the interview.

—Susan House, at her job interview

("I'm fat," House said [Bennett 2001, D3])

Chris, who manages the Giorgio Armani store in Costa Mesa,
California, had a problem. Her young sales associate was in
the habit of only reluctantly showing up for work and spending
the day socializing rather than selling. Since it happened most
of the time, Chris was frustrated. Should she write him a threatening memo, embarrass him at the next staff meeting, or wait for
his performance review to take action? To her credit, Chris did
none of the above. Instead, she decided to meet with him one-on-
one—face-to-face—and look into his eyes.

"One day I pulled him aside and said: 'You know, you can be
something. It could start in this job here today. You're letting your
life pass you by.'" Through the magic of eye contact, Chris managed to convince the young man that her words were true. The
visual connection paid off, and within a month he became the
best salesperson in her store. Instead of using a written warning,
Chris convinced with her eyes.

Eye contact is a visual connection made as one person peers

into the eyes of another. A highly emotional link is established as two people simultaneously look into each other's eyes. Perhaps because the retina is an outgrowth of the forebrain, peering into someone else's eyes is not unlike seeing into the mind itself. This may be why the sacred Eye of Horus, the all-seeing Utchat of Ancient Egypt, had so many complex meanings as a symbol of protection and of the sun and the moon.

One of the main symbols of Hindu theology is the "third eye," which sits in the middle of the sacred forehead of Shiva, who is worshiped as both the restorer and destroyer of worlds. In the business world, we saw how Chris's eyes restored her young associate's attitude and productivity. As with Shiva, however, gaze may also destroy.

On October 24, 2001, at his Houston, Texas, headquarters, Enron's new president, Greg Whalley, abruptly walked into the conference room. He "shot a look" across its oblong table at chief financial officer, Andrew Fastow, and said, "You're no longer CFO, effective right now" (Eichenwald 2005, 5). Stunned, Mr. Fastow shook his head in disbelief and started to reply. But Mr. Whalley just held up a pronated palm (palm facing downward) to silence the ex-CFO, and turned his face and eyes away dismissively. In the clearest of nonverbal terms, it was a done deal. The boss's averted eyes had said, "You're fired."

As the above example shows, in the business world, what the eyes give they can also take away. Showing personal involvement, gaze can be both a restorer and a destroyer of worlds. This chapter examines our paired, golf-ball-size organs of vision, whose movements, condition, pupils, and lid positions reveal a great deal about emotions, convictions, health, and moods. We have an amazing ability to gaze into associates' eyes to gauge their true feelings. What is visual *cutoff*, and what does it say on the job? How does eye contact in a meeting in Japan differ from that given in a meeting in Mexico, Russia, or China? When you look at colleagues in the boardroom, how long should you look? In finding the answers to these questions, you will learn to see into a co-worker's brain through the windows of his or her eyes—and learn what your own eyes might be giving away.

EYE CONTACT IN STARBUCKS

What do Alex, Millard, and Stephan have in common? All three love coffee, all frequent Starbucks, and all would like more eye contact served up with their brew. About his own busy Starbucks in downtown Seattle, Alex complained, "This is one of those places where employees love to chat and laugh loudly among themselves while customers wait for eye contact to place their order" (S. 2007).

Millard, in turn, lamented, "In recent years some Starbucks employees haven't even bothered to acknowledge me or make eye contact when I'm ordering. I find that rude and insensitive" (S. 2008). Last, comparing his Starbucks to the espresso bars he'd visited in Italy, Stephan wrote, "Even if you are a complete stranger, the moment you walk into the [Italian] store, the barista behind the counter will establish eye contact—and ask straight[away] what coffee you would like" (Richter 2008).

None of the three consumers had complaints about the coffee at Starbucks, only about the way it was served—without the magical spark of eye contact. As their comments suggest, withholding gaze in the workplace can be bad for business. When employees don't look, you assume they don't care, so you go elsewhere. Coffee leaves a better taste in your mouth when baristas care enough to greet you with welcoming eyes.

Eye contact varies around the world in duration and strength. In the United States listeners are encouraged to gaze directly into a speaker's eyes. Doing business in Arabic nations, one should expect even more penetrating—and lengthier—gazes. In Japan, on the other hand, listeners are taught to focus on a speaker's neck in order to avoid direct eye contact. On an international business team, an Egyptian may find his Japanese counterpart's lowered eyes disconcerting, while in Japan an Arab's direct gaze may seem too intense. (For more on cultural variation in eye messages, see "When in Rome . . ." page 35.)

As primates, human beings are extremely observant of where others may be looking. Anthropologists, in fact, think the whites of our eyes evolved so the dark pupils and colored irises would more accurately disclose direction of gaze. From across a room we can tell with great accuracy when someone is looking our way. In courtship there's the magical connection known as love at first sight, and on the opposite side of the coin is the aggressive bar-room stare that has led to many a brawl. They're only eyes, after all, but for human primates, where eyes point truly matters.

At a doctor's office patients regularly glance up from magazines to monitor the pupils and irises of others in the waiting room. Though we consciously try to control where our own eyes hover, they have "minds of their own" and glance where they will. In staff meetings we feel compelled to look at eyes, hand gestures, and snack foods. Our primate brain finds these among the top three most compelling items to watch. We notice a co-worker's latte, for instance, which speaks of food, but give her cell phone barely a glance. We check where her eyes go and watch how her hands move as attentively as lowland gorillas monitor each other's hands and eyes in their zoo enclosure. In both habitats, it's less a meeting of minds than a reading of nonverbal clues and connotations.

DISCONNECTING WITH "CUTOFF"

"I have a question about eye contact," Adena asked me in an e-mail. As a consultant, I'm often asked by individual employees to comment on their own and on co-workers' body language. "I've started a new job and my first day (yesterday) coincides with another member of our technical team (a woman) who also started yesterday. Whenever the three of us are standing together, my boss looks more directly at her than at me. Is this a sign of his disapproval and possible dislike of me, and his favoritism of her? I hate to start a new job on such a negative note, but I feel really rejected when he does this. Could you lend some thoughts as to whether this is disapproval or perhaps he just feels more comfortable with her? I'm not sure" (Adena 2001a).

In my e-mail back, I wrote Adena that she may indeed have been a victim of preferential treatment on the job. That it was visible on her first day of work was a premonition of not-so-nice things to come. I asked her to elaborate. She replied:

> He and I had a one-on-one conversation in his office my first day. This was such an important day for me. I was eager to get off on a good note. My colleague and I started the same day and he met with her first. He spent a lot of time with her and then when he met with me, he was so strange. He kept looking down and away from me. Then, he kept shuffling papers around and would stand up and walk over to his desk. After this, he was in a hurry to finish our meeting and kind of nonverbally tossed me out of the office. I guess I'm feeling like the yucky stepchild in this boss/employee relationship when compared to my colleague. After this meeting, the next day, is when he approached both of us and started a conversation but looked at her the entire time. How strange! (Adena 2001b)

I get more questions about eye contact than about any other nonverbal cues. Adena's case was clearly one of being on the wrong side of preferential treatment. First, eye contact from her boss was markedly less than what her colleague had received. Second, the neglect was repeated, showing a degree of consistency in the pattern. Third, the rude eye behavior was accompanied by equally rude paper shuffling, walking away, and hurried mannerisms intended to cut the meeting short. Adena got neither equal attention nor equal time from her new boss, and it showed.

I know how Adena felt. In my own work experience, I once had a boss who gazed at my mouth and that of others when he spoke and never looked into our eyes. We all noticed John's peculiar mouth regard and commented on it behind his back. What in the world did it mean?

To the primate mind, not looking usually translates as "not liking." "Thus," primatologist Stuart Altmann writes, "one interpretation of avoiding visual contact—which has been described in rhesus, baboons, bonnet macaques, [and] gorillas—is that it is a means of avoiding interactions" (Altmann 1967, 332). In the office, as Adena's case attests, a boss's avoidant eye contact telegraphs an avoidant frame of mind. In my own boss's case, however, John's mouth gaze was less unfriendly than merely odd. He avoided everyone's eyes equally, a pattern that's normal in Hong Kong and Tokyo but rare in the United States.

An especially telling form of office gaze aversion is *cutoff*. Picture yourself meeting with a colleague to share ideas on a new-product launch. Midway through your proposal you notice the listener's face turn completely away from you. Her eyes no longer meet yours, but angle ninety degrees off to your left. Her cutoff is a clear sign that she dislikes or disagrees with your plan. As long as her face is turned so far away, there's little chance of accord. Before progress can be made, you need to bring her face and eyes back by asking if she has anything to add to your idea. You need to clear up objections face-to-face before they have a chance to fester after the meeting.

HER EYES AVOIDED US

In his article "Let's Improve Our Office Demeanor," Dr. Arnold Melnick complained about the poor communication he'd experienced in his own doctor's office. When Dr. Melnick arrived for his appointment, the waiting room was empty, as was the reception desk at the front of the office. Another patient arrived and took a seat near Dr. Melnick. Both patients then had to wait for ten minutes until the receptionist finally returned and sat down at her desk.

"She assiduously avoided looking at us," Dr. Melnick wrote, "but was busy, officious, bustling with paperwork and making telephone calls—never acknowledging any of us patients. Not even a 'Good afternoon'" (Melnick 2007, 14).

When he approached the desk to check in, the receptionist wrote down his name, told him she'd have to get his chart, and turned her eyes back to her paperwork. She impatiently dismissed him before the appointment had begun.

A physician himself, Dr. Melnick was prompted to write an article for the American Osteopathic Association's official newsletter, *The DO,* about the poor office communication he'd received. He concluded that doctor's office personnel should always greet patients with signals—verbal and nonverbal—that say, "Welcome to our office." Even if you're on the phone, he reminded, you can make eye contact, smile, and nod a hello. A simple message, "Yes, I see you," would have kept a happier Arnold Melnick from penning his complaint.

WHEN IN ROME . . .

When you sight-read eyes across a conference table, be mindful of where in the world that table is. Our examples thus far have pertained mostly to business in the United States, but when you watch eyes in Italy, for example, you will notice differences in eye behavior, and in China the differences will be greater still. An American on assignment in Rome may feel uncomfortable when an Italian counterpart across the table seems to repeatedly look—or even to stare. Since it's the norm for Italians to give more direct eye contact in business meetings than Americans give, consider the enhanced gaze you receive in Italy a positive sign of interest, honesty, and rapport. Longer glances there are simply the norm. Being stared at across a table in Beijing, however, could be a negative signal of anger, challenge, or open hostility. You'll definitely feel you're no longer in Rome.

"When [Chinese] people get angry," writes James Chan, Ph.D., author of 18 *Practical Tips on Working with Your Chinese Partners,* "they tend to maintain steady eye contact. Otherwise, they look elsewhere or appear nonchalant while talking." Though you may feel ignored or excluded at a meeting when your Asian counterpart gazes off into the distance, looks away to the side, or glances down at notes while speaking, it's not really a problem. Indeed, gaze avoidance is not a concern in Chinese business; it's a custom.

"For the Chinese," Chan advises, "lack of steady eye contact doesn't indicate a lack of attention or respect. On the contrary . . . steady eye contact is viewed as inappropriate . . . [and] sometimes viewed as a gesture of challenge or defiance" (Chan 2009). In the United States we're taught to make direct eye contact in business settings to show interest, respect, and truthfulness. Such is not the case in China, where a direct gaze may be taken as disrespectful, especially when given by a subordinate to a boss. The superior will decode visual contact as a sign of direct challenge to his or her authority. Thus, in China it's appropriate and even expected in meetings that you listen and speak without looking directly into colleagues' eyes.

Americans may misread the lack of eye contact as evidence of inattention or disinterest. They may feel their suggestions and ideas are not being understood or are being discounted by Chinese colleagues across the table. Again, it's a custom—politeness—and not a cause for alarm. Return the favor by moderating and softening your own gaze in return. When in China, do with your eyes what Chinese eyes do.

If Chinese eye rituals are challenging to American business-people, Japan's eye rituals are more enigmatic still. "A Japanese businessman," Kazuo Nishiyama writes in his book *Doing Business with Japan,* "frequently shifts his eyes during a difficult negotiation session because he feels that sustained eye contact might be over-bearing and rude. But this shifting of the eyes may well be inter-preted by his American business associate as an indication of dishonesty or disinterest" (Nishiyama 2000, 23).

As in China, minor differences in where one's eyes go at a meet-ing can engender major misunderstandings. Matters are further complicated by the Japanese custom of bowing. The polite Japa-nese bow—bending forward at the waist with the hands and arms held down beside the body—includes an implicit rule of breaking eye contact. The unstated expectation is that when you first meet and greet in person, you both should stare down at the floor. For Americans who are taught to step forward, make eye contact, and reach out an open hand, such a bow may be as hard to give as to receive. After all, eye contact and a handshake are as natural to Americans as ice cream and apple pie. (More natural to the Japa-nese are *uirō*, or dessert rice cakes, and *kakigōri*, shaved ice.) But as Jon Alston and Isao Takei write in their book, *Japanese Business Cul-ture and Practices,* in Japan, "introductions and shaking hands are accompanied with lowered eyes because prolonged eye contact is seen as impolite. Do not feel insulted with others' lack of eye con-tact. They are merely showing respect by avoiding too much eye contact" (Alston and Takei 2005, 39).

Differences in eye regard can be deceiving. In Japan a steady, eye-to-eye gaze is often seen as aggressive, belligerent, rude, and insistent upon equality (Nishiyama 2000, 23). Across a board-room table in Istanbul, however, the opposite is true. Strong eye contact while you listen to Turkish colleagues is regarded as a sign of sincerity. For an American businessman in Turkey, if eye con-tact received at a board meeting feels a bit too strong, the closer proximity of eye-to-eye contact after the meeting can feel even more intense. In stand-up conversations after the formal sit-down meeting, Turkish men move closer together than American men are accustomed to standing. The usual eighteen to twenty-four inches between faces for informal talk in the United States may be reduced to barely twelve inches apart in Turkey. Yet while the proximity may feel too close for comfort, Americans are advised not to avert eyes or back away, since doing so would seem un-friendly or rude.

In the wild world among our closest animal cousins, the chim-panzees, primatologist Jane Goodall found that adults do not engage in long or sustained eye gaze with each other. In the hu-man world of business, however, eye contact varies from culture to culture. Americans in Italy should maintain strong eye contact while speaking to convey sincerity and honesty. In Russia direct eye contact and a firm handshake suggest strength. In France moderate-level eye contact is recommended for best rapport. With your Mexican colleagues, infrequent gaze contact is the norm; a prolonged, direct gaze at a meeting in Mexico may signal disre-spect, challenge, or a hard sell. As business becomes more global, . subtle differences in how you give and receive eye contact across a conference table will matter more than ever.

EYEBALL TO EYEBALL

At the beginning of this chapter, we saw that a highly emotional link is established as two people simultaneously look into each other's eyes. Peering into someone else's eyes is like seeing into the soul itself. Eyes are so emotional that you will no doubt expe-rience some discomfort as you sight-read eye messages in the office. Thus, I'll soon suggest a specific method for reading our paired organs of sight (see below, "How to Read Eyes across a Confer-ence Table").

Human infants respond to eyes from the second week of life. They alert to and show strong interest in paired, rounded eye spots projected side-by-side on a screen. Babies will not show interest, however, when the spots are projected in vertical alignment, with one dark spot placed above the other. Vertically placed spots don't register in baby's brain as eyes, only as spots. This natural fascination for paired, horizontally configured human eyes remains with us throughout life. In the workplace, eye actions are dramatized on the stage defined by a conference table. Above the tabletop, with our lower bodies sequestered below, we are programmed to focus attention almost entirely on eyes, faces, shoulders, and hands. As the boardroom drama unfolds, eyes are the lead actors.

Though there are marked cultural differences, the emotional "spark" we feel as we make eye contact with each other is universal. The magic of eyeball-to-eyeball sets off physiological arousal in the nervous system that can be measured as spikes in the body's heart rate, blood pressure, and brain-wave activity. We respond to the arousal by breaking eye contact to reduce our physiological and psychological levels of stress. Around the world, human beings employ a generally alternating pattern of gazing at someone, then gazing away. The cycle repeats as a conversation continues. As we have seen, time spent in direct-gaze mode is longer in Turkey than it is in Japan, but in no society do people continually stare, nor do they avoid eye-to-eye gaze altogether.

As with my former boss's mouth gaze, however, there are odd exceptions to the rule. "I was speaking to a woman about a situation where someone we both know sneakily managed to slough a task onto me that she had volunteered to do," Megan wrote me in an e-mail. "The entire time I was speaking to this woman—easily two to three minutes—her eyes were totally closed! It was the most bizarre thing I've ever seen. Her face never left looking directly at me but her eyes were completely closed—she never opened them for so much as a second. I'm thinking that this was a defensive cue, but to have them closed for so long struck me as very odd. I noticed it immediately and couldn't take my eyes off her, waiting to see how long they would stay shut. I don't think I heard a word she was saying because of this eye behavior" (Megan 2001, personal comm.). Indeed, there are emotional as well as cultural differences in eye contact, and both clearly show. Megan was confronted by what physicians call a zebra case, a symptom so bizarre as to defy diagnosis.

HOW TO READ EYES ACROSS A CONFERENCE TABLE

To read eyes at a meeting, the first thing to look for is eye color. Closely examine the color of the round, pigmented, contractile membrane of the eye. Is it pale blue, blue, blue-green, green, greenish brown, light brown, or dark brown? The color tells you nothing about intentions or moods, but explicitly noting eye color will get you past the emotions that make sight-reading eyes such a challenge. Look for the color first, but be cautious and don't look for too long. (Eye contact is so emotional you may be unable to recall the color of your own boss's eyes.)

Next, examine the size of the pupil, the dark, circular opening inside the iris. Unlike eye color, pupil size has a lot to say about mood. A small or constricted pupil shows that a colleague is in a generally relaxed state of mind. Perhaps she just got back from lunch and is in rest-and-digest mode. A larger, dilated pupil is often a sign of emotional arousal or excitement. Your colleague may have had more than the usual amount of coffee before the meeting. Or perhaps an inflammatory remark by the boss set off alarm bells and triggered the fight-or-flight response. Watch for changes in pupil size to predict if a co-worker is about to fall asleep at the table from boredom (very constricted), or is preparing to challenge your new business plan (very dilated).

Pupils are reliable mood indicators in the workplace because their cues are involuntary and hard to control at will. Their size acts in response to emotional stimuli, or light, and cannot be constricted or dilated on purpose. Pupils automatically constrict before sleep, and they enlarge in excitement through a release of noradrenaline into the sympathetic nervous system. Whether constricted or dilated, their small size makes watching them across a table, especially in colleagues with dark-pigmented irises, something of a challenge. But judging from card players who read pupils as tell signs (enlarged pupils signal a good poker hand), their messages are available to those who watch. Unlike poker players, who know opponents read pupils in their line of work, business-people seldom wear dark glasses in the boardroom.

Once you've gotten over your emotional resistance to reading eyes, you can watch for additional messages that eyes emit in face-to-face meetings. First is an involuntary shift in movement to the right or left side. Known as a CLEM (acronym for *conjugate lateral eye movement*), the sideward shift suggests a listener is actively processing the information you shared with the group. It is a positive sign your suggestion or new idea hasn't fallen on deaf ears.

Unlike the usually negative cutoff cue described earlier, in which a co-worker turns his or her head fully away to one side to disagree, in CLEMs only the eyes move while the head itself stays perfectly still. The CLEM is a nonverbal response, often to a verbal question, in which both eyes move sideward, to the right or left, in tandem. Easier than pupil size to see, CLEMs signal information processing, reflection, and thought.

In his classic study of CLEMs in mathematicians, Stevan Harnad (1972) noted that rightward eye movement associated well with symbolic thinking, while leftward movement associated with visual thinking. Left-movers were thought to be more creative. At a staff meeting, watching CLEMs can be both entertaining and instructive. Since they're an index of brain-hemispheric activation

CLEMs *signal reflection and thought.*

(Gur 1975), sideward eye movements give you some indication of how colleagues feel about your comments and thoughts.

As you sit at your meeting table monitoring irises, pupils, and CLEMs, also watch for "flashbulb eyes." This very visible facial cue shows that strong feelings have come to the fore. As a nonverbal sign, flashbulb eyes are an involuntary and dramatic widening of the eyes in situations of intense emotion such as anger, surprise, shock, and fear. Maximal opening of the eyelids (in medical terms, dilation of the *palpebral fissure*) clearly shows the roundness, curvature, and in some cases even protrusion of the eyeballs themselves.

When we're truly surprised or fearful, rather than feigning the emotion for effect (as in a conversation), two involuntary visceral muscles in our eyelids—the *superior* and *inferior tarsals*—widen the eye slits to make both eyes appear noticeably larger, rounder, and whiter. Like enlarged pupils, the flashbulb-eyes signal is controlled by impulses of the nervous system's fight-or-flight division. Because flashbulb eyes are hard to produce at will, they're all the more trustworthy as nonverbal cues. Powerful emotions of terror and rage, for example, register first in the eyes before the body mobilizes to withdraw or lash out. As I advise in seminars for superior court judges, seeing flashbulb eyes in a courtroom is a preincident warning sign that means it's time to alert the bailiff. Since physical attack may be imminent, a defendant, witness, lawyer, or judge may be in danger. Seen in the boardroom, flashbulb eyes may mean that something you've said may come under attack.

Though we may consciously widen our eyes, full dilation of the pupil enlists involuntary responses from the tarsal muscles. These muscles of the upper and lower eyelids are activated by the fight-or-flight division of the nervous system, working through parts of the spinal cord known as the *superior cervical ganglia*. When you see unusually wide eyes with whites visible entirely around the iris, take note—take cover.

In his book *Blink: The Power of Thinking Without Thinking* (2005), Malcolm Gladwell looks at the potency and accuracy of intuition and first impressions—which happen "in the blink of an eye." In the boardroom, you should look to the blink itself for intuition on what colleagues may be thinking before they tell you—if they ever do—concretely in words.

A blink is a rapid closing and opening of the eyes. In the workplace, blink rate reflects psychological arousal in the manner of a lie detector or polygraph test. The normal, resting blink rate of a human is twenty closures per minute, with the average blink lasting one-quarter of a second (Karson 1992). Significantly faster rates may reflect emotional stress aroused in the fight-or-flight response.

Watch for obviously faster blinking rates in colleagues to gauge how excited—or exercised—they are about agenda items on the table. Those who blink slowly may not be as emotionally invested as those who speed up. In mental patients, eye-blink rates rise with anxious or tense topics, and with changes to a new topic (Kanfer 1960). I've observed this to be generally the case in business meetings, with the proviso that bosses and managers often have lower blinking rates. As leaders, they tend to have more control and are therefore less threatened by novel ideas than are lower-ranking employees.

Like other seemingly simple body movements, blinking is hardly simple. Our blink rate is controlled at the basic level by paleocircuits of the ancestral amphibian brain (Givens 2009). Also known as the midbrain, this ancient part of our neuroanatomy enabled ancient forebears to see—and blink—above the waterline of Devonian seas. Out of water in open air, the act of blinking kept amphibian eyes from drying out.

But human blinking is also affected by emotional responses. We blink faster when excited because eyelid movements reflect bodily arousal levels established by the brain stem's primeval *reticular activating system (RAS)*. Emotions stimulate the RAS to act on our midbrain's *substantia nigra*, which releases the excitatory chemical dopamine to the amphibian brain's *superior colliculi* (Karson 1992, 417). In a nutshell, we bat our eyelids faster when we feel tense at a meeting, especially when we stall, overstate our case, or outright lie to colleagues across the table. Like GEICO's gecko, the ancestral amphibian in our midbrain can't hold its tongue.

A good deal of our primate brain's cortex is dedicated to vision. Where eyes look is a clear sign of where your colleagues' attention lies. There's no better way to gauge what's on a co-worker's mind than to watch his or her eyes. Line of sight across—and eye movements above—the board table clearly show where associates stand on issues. At meetings, the average worker is so absorbed by spoken and written words that unspoken messages remain largely out of sight. Sight-reading eyes across the conference table will make your comprehension far above average.

In the next chapter, your eyes will learn to read the messages hands give in the workplace. You will learn to garner rapport with palm-up gestures, and to use palm-down cues to appear more confident in boardroom debates.

The Business at Hand

His hands rose, fluttered like wounded birds a few inches above the surface of his desk, slowly came back to a landing.

—George C. Chesbro, *Shadow of a Broken Man*

Microsoft CEO Steve Ballmer is a self-acknowledged *table pounder*. A table pounder is one who slaps office furniture with the flat of an open palm for emphasis. It's rather like using a judge's gavel to impose order in court. The authoritative or angry hand comes down sharply on a flat surface to make a firm point. Viewers know instantly what the gesture means, and are glad it came down on a table instead of a head.

An able table pounder from decades ago was Nikita Khrushchev, first secretary of the Communist Party of the former Soviet Union. In the 1960s Khrushchev had a habit of pounding on his desk to disrupt meetings of the United Nations General Assembly. The gesture he's most famous for is slamming the desktop with his shoe. On September 29, 1960, he brought his right shoe down on the desktop to interrupt a speech by British prime minister Harold Macmillan, with whom he disagreed.

Roots of table pounding run deep. In preschool children, the *pound* gesture is "a sharp blow by one hand against the other immobile hand or against an object such as a table" (Brannigan and

Humphries 1972, 61). *Slap ground* is an aggressive gesture used by langurs and savannah baboons, and used as a threat gesture by our closest animal relative, the chimpanzee. Like Khrushchev's shoe slam, the chimp's palm-down slap shows dramatic assertion and attitude.

It's the same in business. To show conviction to colleagues across a board table, use *palm-down* gestures to emphasize your key speaking points. Without actually striking the tabletop, pronate your open palm—flip it down, parallel to the table's surface—and proffer it as a sign. Reach the gesture forward, while moving it up and down like a baton, to drive home your most important ideas. Without realizing why, listeners will sense you have greater confidence in your words.

You've seen the palm-down gesture on political talk shows like *Meet the Press.* As pundits and politicians argue great issues of the day, they authoritatively pronate (rotate one or both hands into slap-ground position), reach out, and gavel with palm-down hands on the air. At staff meetings you, too, can reach out with palm-down gestures to show you mean business.

A gesture I call *hand-behind-head* bespeaks the opposite of conviction, namely, the feeling of uncertainty. Be suspicious when colleagues make sudden hand-behind-head movements. Here's an example of a world-famous newscaster who inadvertently tipped his hand, so to speak. On December 29, 2000, while explaining his network's flawed projection for the winner of the U.S. presidential contest in Florida on *The Tonight Show* with Jay Leno—declaring Al Gore, then George W. Bush, the victor—then NBC *Nightly News* anchor Tom Brokaw lifted his right hand up and reached back to scratch the crown of his coiffed hairdo. Without realizing it, Tom had given the classic hand-behind-head signal of perplexity. Millions of viewers watched the normally unflappable Brokaw squirm as he displayed his chagrin.

Touching, scratching, or holding the back of the neck or head with an open palm is a telltale sign of uncertainty, mental conflict, or frustration. The gesture telegraphs an unresolved issue to explore. In Mr. Brokaw's case, the televised hand-behind-head reflected personal shame—a keen feeling of mental unease—over NBC's colossal mistake.

At a conference table, should your boss give the hand-behind-head sign as you explain your proposal, the gesture means you probably have more explaining to do. Controlled by emotional centers in the boss's brain, the hand movement suggests a conflicted state of mind. When you see the hand come back down to the tabletop, it shows the boss has mentally shifted gears and may be in a more receptive mood.

For hand gestures, think of the conference table as a stage. A conference table is a platform to facilitate face-to-face meetings. It is the corporate "level playing field" upon which speakers address colleagues on matters of business. Nonverbally, the board table is a flatland, a territory in which to exchange hand gestures of harmony or discord, offense or defense. In this chapter we will see how hand shapes, positions, movements, and gestures wage war on its surface and in the airspace above.

How do hand gestures enhance comprehension? What does it mean when a colleague stops gesturing with his hands? Why are

Hand-behind-head suggests a conflicted state of mind.

palm-up cues generally calming, comforting, and conciliatory? How do *mime* cues enhance the comprehension of your words? To learn how hands speak in the office, read on.

MIDDLE-FINGER-SPEAK

In her graduation speech to students at Columbia University Business School on May 15, 2005, PepsiCo president and then-CFO Indra Nooyi likened the five fingers of her hand to the five land areas of Africa, Asia, Latin America, Europe, and the United States (Nooyi 2005). Seeing the world in the digits of a hand evolved from the childhood chats Ms. Nooyi had with her mother and sister at their home in Madras, India. They looked at one another's hands, noticed differences in finger size and shape, and talked about how, despite the differences, fingers "worked together to create a wonderful tool"—the human hand.

In Ms. Nooyi's anatomical mapping, the little finger is Africa. While the continent itself is huge, Africa's economic standing on the world stage is small. "And yet, when our little finger hurts," Nooyi told the graduates, "it affects the whole hand."

The thumb, our thickest and strongest digit, is Asia, because Asia is a powerful player in the world's economy. Next, the index finger we point with is Europe, the geographical region that "pointed the way for Western civilization and the laws we use in conducting global business."

Our wedding-ring finger, meanwhile, embodies the combined areas of South America and Latin America. Ms. Nooyi finds a romantic theme in the region's hot, passionate, and sensuous dance movements in the mambo, samba, and tango. Finally, our longest or middle finger is the United States. "As the longest of the fingers," Nooyi explained in her graduation speech, "it really stands out"—just as the United States stands out as the major player in global business today."

After mapping the five fingers geographically as continents, Indra Nooyi pointed out how the United States has been guilty of waving its middle finger around in a negative way as an obscene gesture. Instead of reaching out to the world with an open hand, America gives it the finger.

Digitus impudicus—the indecent finger—is a widespread gesture of sexual insult. Simply "the finger," as it's known in the United States, it traces back to at least ancient Rome, to the evil emperor Caligula. Today there are numerous photos on the Internet of former U.S. president George W. Bush reportedly giving the finger in public. Seeing the pictures, viewers from abroad might assume it's directed at them as a threat.

Giving or seeming to give the finger is a minor gesture that sends a major message. In September 2008, Ms. Nooyi, fifty-two, who by this point occupied the office of PepsiCo CEO, was named the most powerful woman in business by *Fortune* magazine for the third year in a row. Her earlier, 2005 remarks at Columbia—which alluded to a bullying American foreign policy—were a telling sign of the times: "Unfortunately, I think this is how the rest of the world looks at the U.S. right now," Nooyi had said. "Not as part of the hand—giving strength and purpose to the rest of the fingers—but, instead, scratching our nose and sending a far different signal" (Nooyi 2005).

CRUZ STUCK UP HER HAND

In the business world, colleagues will remember your hand gestures long after your words fade away. Giving co-workers a *halt hand,* for example, to quiet or shush them—to keep them from talking back to you at a meeting—will stay lodged in memory far longer than accompanying words.

The meaning of the halt-hand gesture—"I hold you back"—shows in an arm held straight out with the palm facing the person you shush. This is the hand signal traffic officers use to stop vehicles at intersections. Used in a meeting, the militant halt hand is just as authoritative. An arm stiffens as an aggressively pronated palm reaches in your direction to "push" you back. Given in the context of mild or strong anger, you'll forever remember the halt hand as an unwanted, unappreciated, unfriendly command.

In September 2007 Zoe Cruz, then copresident of Morgan Stanley, used her palm to shush a board member who tried to interrupt her in a committee meeting. "Cruz stuck up her hand," *New York* magazine reported, "and snapped, 'I'm not finished yet!'" (Hagan 2008).

Voted one of the world's most powerful businesswomen in 2006 by *Fortune* magazine, Zoe Cruz showed an increasingly defensive posture after Morgan Stanley's $3.7 billion loss in 2007, a dramatic hemorrhage that happened on her watch as copresident. Ms. Cruz's defensiveness showed in anger. Instead of taking personal responsibility for the loss, Cruz, noted *The Wall Street Journal*, "instead lashed out at fellow employees in a series of meetings about the losses, raising questions about her management style" (Smith et al. 2007, B1).

Zoe Cruz's body language before, during, and after the financial hemorrhage had been sending the wrong signals to co-workers and board members alike. Her imperious, confrontational management style was such that Morgan Stanley CEO John Mack hired a personal coach to work with her. Cruz was accused of sometimes using an overly emotional, cracking voice at meetings, and of crying to get her way. As the billion-dollar losses became known around the office, Ms. Cruz, who was not a frequent smoker, repeatedly left the building for cigarette breaks and got into heated arguments with staff. She sometimes publicly displayed a "disharmonious" posture in relations with her copresident, Robert Scully, whom she verbally contradicted in meetings.

Rather than cultivate allies, Zoe Cruz's demeanor alienated many of Morgan Stanley's most powerful board members. When the board met by telephone on November 29, 2007, to consider Cruz's firing, few argued in her favor. Indeed, Ms. Cruz was gone before she herself knew it, two months after the committee meeting in which she'd imperiously stuck up her hand.

How to Hold a Business Card

In the business world rapport can be established or broken by the way you hold an object in your hand. This is especially true of business cards.

When a Japanese businessman hands you his card, you should not take it in one hand and summarily stuff it into your pocket. To hold the card in a single hand, give it a cursory glance, and stow it in a pocket shows disrespect. Also, while it is acceptable in the United States to hold a business card in a casual way, gripped between the thumb and side of your forefinger, it is not okay in Japan.

In Japan you are expected to receive a business card reverently. You should grasp it with both hands, touch it with the sensitive tactile pads of your thumb in tandem with at least two fingertips of each hand, and give it a careful reading. In an even more reverent display you'd involve all five fingers, again of both hands, in the holding. The more tactile hands-on attention you give the business card, the more respect you show. Holding it reverently signals that you've not just received the card but taken ownership.

In consulting work for Hallmark Cards, Inc., in Kansas City, I observed shoppers in greeting-card stores in Missouri and Washington State. I discovered what I call the *decision grip*. The decision grip is a manner of grasping an object securely between the sensitive fingertips and the palm. As a "proprietary clasp," it is a clear indication that a customer has decided to take possession of a greeting card and make a purchase.

The decision grip is a nonverbal sign showing your mind has decided to buy. After an exploratory waiting period reflected by holding the card tentatively—between the tactile pad of your thumb and the less sensitive side of your forefinger—you unwittingly shift the item to decision-grip mode. Doing so maximizes the tactile connection between the card and the nerve-rich pads of your fingertips, as if it were in the palm of your hand as a belonging.

In Japan you should hold another's business card as if it were a greeting card, which in many respects it is. Once you've thoroughly read its message—in the greeting-card business the message is known as a "sentiment"—place the card securely in your wallet, purse, or briefcase. Respecting the card shows respect for the person.

OUTGOING HANDS

If a hand can show arrogance, as in Zoe Cruz's case, it can also show an interest in people. Extending a friendly open palm—either as a gesture or an invitation to shake hands—can release your inner extrovert. In psychology an extrovert is a person who displays concern for other people. On the reverse side of the coin is the introvert, a person who directs attention within, into the self, and is less likely to reach out to others. In business those who reach out with hands have an advantage over those who keep hands to themselves, concealed in pockets, folded in laps, or hidden beneath desks.

"So get out there, mix, speak more often, and connect with both your team and others, deploying all the energy and personality you can muster." Thus wrote Jack and Suzy Welch in their advice column for *BusinessWeek* magazine (Welch and Welch 2008,

92). The Welches were answering a question from an anonymous woman whose boss told her she needed to display a "stronger personality" if she wanted a promotion. The problem, the Atlanta business executive confessed, was that she was a "natural introvert."

Introverted employees in large organizations, the Welches note, often have more problems excelling than do more extroverted staff members who are able to connect and motivate colleagues on the job. As an anthropologist, I've observed an easy way to project your outgoing side: Simply move your hands more. In studies of videotaped boardroom meetings, I found that women who moved their hands above the table as they spoke commanded more attention and were taken more seriously than women who spoke with their hands out of sight in laps under tabletops.

In the research I did for Unilever on hand creams (see chapter 1), I learned that human beings have a special appreciation for hand shapes, movements, and gestures. We notice and take hands very seriously because we are primates. A primate brain's temporal lobes are highly attuned to the organs with which we gesticulate, grip, grasp, and shake hands. In the Unilever study I discovered that we are especially attentive to signs of grooming, gender, and age in the hands we see. Calluses, dirt under fingernails, and age spots, for example, register as unsightly, negative signs. That hands so fascinate us explains why Michelangelo painted, Rodin sculpted, and Annie Liebovitz photographed graceful hands on behalf of art. In the conference room, reach out and move your well-groomed hands in the interest of your success.

HANDSHAKES

In business today, the handshake is used as a worldwide gesture for meeting, greeting, and sealing a deal. It is a ritualized gripping of another's hand, with one or more up-and-down (or, in Texas,

sideways) motions followed by a quick release. As we've seen, since
the fingertips and palmar surface of the hand are exquisitely sensitive, the shake itself can be deeply personal. We instantly feel
the warmth or coolness, dryness or moistness, and firmness or
weakness of another's grip. Sensory input from a hand's thermal
and pressure receptors to the brain's parietal sensory area can be
intense, especially in courtship. From the parietal lobe, the handshake's message travels to deeper areas of the limbic system for an
emotional interpretation to judge how the shake felt.

If you travel to France on business, be prepared to shake hands
dozens of times a day. Office workers in Paris may shake in the
morning to greet colleagues, and in the afternoon to say good-bye
to them. Outside vendors and technicians will shake hands with
everyone present when they enter or leave an office. Contrast this
with the Japanese practice of giving few intraoffice handshakes in
favor of polite bows of the head. In Islamic nations it is strictly
taboo for men to shake hands in public with women. So, while the
handshake has become a worldwide gesture in business, you should
learn cultural protocols on shaking hands before you travel.

Since in much of the world a handshake is both a visual and a
tactile index of your concern for other people, a rule of thumb is
not to hold back. In North America, Latin America, and Europe,
take the lead, step forward, and shake a hand. Shaking will raise
your extrovert quotient and show colleagues you care about them
as people. In Asia, South Asia, and the Middle East, handshak-
ing may be more nuanced. Learn the cultural rules in these re-
gions before stepping forward with your hand up and out. An
Indian *namaste,* with your palms and fingers pressed together in
front of your chest, given with a slight bow; or a Muslim salaam,
in which your right hand touches your forehead, also with a slight
bow, may be better signals to send.

Wherever in the world you conduct business, don't hide your
hands behind you or keep them out of sight. Show them to attract

notice to yourself and to emphasize your ideas. Hands are great ambassadors to those in business you don't know well. In their unspoken language, which is both mysterious yet understood by all, hands speak strongly on your behalf.

UNIVERSAL GESTURES

If handshakes are widespread but not used globally in business, I've found four basic categories of hand gestures, given in every society, that are understood by people everywhere. You'll see these gestures in business settings from Houston to Hong Kong, and their messages are always the same. Wherever you take a meeting, how you move your hands will lead others to perceive you as an *illustrator*, an *explainer*, a *convincer*—or a *fidgeter*.

Mime Cues

As an illustrator you use *mime* cues to depict the size, shape, and location of persons, places, and things. A mime cue is a speaking gesture in which the hands and fingers mimic spatial-temporal relationships of, and among, objects, activities, and events. An illustrator's hands speak figuratively alongside vocal cues.

A typical mime cue is the *walking figure*, in which two fingers "walk" on a desktop to mimic the body's rhythmic, strolling gait. Mime cues also may be used in sequence for storytelling. An example would be miming the physical actions of gathering snow and throwing a snowball as you say, "I pick up snow," "form a snowball," and "throw it at you." Your hands tell the story in tandem with your words.

In her book *Hearing Gesture: How Our Hands Help us Think* (2005), University of Chicago psychologist Susan Goldin-Meadow shows how gestures aid in the comprehension of spoken words and ideas. Using mime cues at a meeting to illustrate a business plan will help colleagues better understand what's on your mind. That the neurological circuits of manual mimicry are as complex as those of speech renders them powerfully expressive. Since they reveal the presence of conceptual thought, mime cues are your most intellectual gestures. Like words, they express narrative thinking, relationships between objects, and associations among ideas. On a body-language grading scale, mime cues earn high marks in face-to-face meetings. Since they improve understanding, use them liberally to illustrate talking points.

For too many years, speech instructors have discouraged students from talking with their hands. Teachers advise that hand movements distract, get in the way, and detract from spoken words. While this may be true for official speeches from formal podiums, it's not the case for staff, business, and board meetings. Talking with your hands aids comprehension, Ms. Goldin-Meadow suggests, because it enlists spatial and nonverbal areas of listeners' brains. Spoken words are processed only in speech centers on the left-hand side of the brain, but the act of speaking and miming together hits both sides of the brain at once.

Palm-up Cues

Unlike an illustrator's gestures, an explainer's hand gestures don't depict objects or mime relationships in space. Explainers' *palm-up* cues make emotional appeals for listener support, cooperation, and understanding. "Palm-up" is a universal gesture made with the fingers extended and the hand rotated to an upward (or *supinated*) position parallel to the ceiling. The uplifted, opened palm is held out as an imploring gesture suggesting a vulnerable side, a nonaggressive stance appealing to listeners as allies rather than as rivals or foes.

Throughout the world palm-up gestures reflect moods of

Use plam-up to reach out to colleagues in a non-aggressive way.

accommodation, congeniality, and humility. Accompanied by palm-showing cues, your ideas, opinions, and remarks seem more concili-iatory than assertive, aggressive, or pointed. Held out to an opponent across a conference table, the proffered palm may, like an olive branch, enlist support as an emblem of peace.

Palm-up cues are culturally universal and rooted in our basically primate nature. According to zoologist Frans de Waal, they're used by our close cousins, the chimpanzees *(Pan troglodytes)*, to beg for food and settle disputes. All a chimp need do to make amends is proffer an upraised palm. Extending an open hand held in up-ward position means the same in the office as it does in the bush: "I mean you no harm."

As an anthropologist I carry a notebook. I've recorded many observations of palm-up gestures appealing for sympathy, plead-ing for favors, and asking for help. Here are some of my favorite examples from my field notes:

- A sales rep appeals to her boss with a palm-up cue: "Do you really want me to fly out to Cleveland tomorrow?"

- A teenager asks to borrow his mother's car using a raised palm to plead: "Please, Mom?"

- In Ghana a tribal woman gestures with lifted palms after hearing that her husband favors polygamy and wants more than one wife: "What can we women do?" she asks hopelessly.

- In the boardroom a CEO appeals to senior staff with a palm-up gesture imploring: "I need your help."

Palm-up is one of the better signs to have in your kitbag of gestures. Use it to reach toward colleagues in a nonaggressive way to bring them psychologically closer. Though coworkers may have reservations about being touched, they appreciate signs showing they're liked and included.

Palm-down Gestures

Convincers use precisely the opposite sign, *palm-down,* with precisely the opposite sense. A convincer gives the more aggressive gesture to drive home a point. Palm-down is an insistent, adamant gesture made with the fingers extended and the hand rotated downward (*pronated*) parallel with the floor. It's the position a hand assumes in a floor push-up.

Palm-down gestures show confidence, assertiveness, and dominance. They contrast with friendlier palm-up cues. Recall the table-pounding gesture of Microsoft's Steve Ballmer. His is a more vehement version of the pronated palm. As a forceful sign, the palm-down beating motion makes your ideas and opinions seem more convincing. Raised and lowered like a judge's gavel, the palm-down cue makes a strong statement when used above a desk or conference table. (You needn't actually pound the tabletop to show conviction.)

The palm-down motion makes your ideas seem more convincing.

Anatomically, a military or floor push-up involves muscles of the shoulder girdle and upper arm, forearm, wrist, and fingers. Braided nerve networks from the cervical and brachial plexuses coordinate the palm-down cue. A primitive motor center in our brain called the *basal ganglia* governs the palm-down gesture, just as it governs the iguana's push-up to a high stand, a display designed to intimidate rivals.

With its reptilian pedigree, cultural expressions of palm-down are prolific. In Greece the pronated *palms thrust* or "double *moutza*" gesture, with the arms extended horizontally and thrust outward, is an insult that says, "Go to hell twice" (Morris 1994, 196). Like the Saudi *hand slap* for "contempt" and the Italian *forearm thrust* used as a sexual insult, moutza gestures incorporate the natural aggressiveness of pronated beating movements.

In the office it's best to use pronated palms strategically and sparingly. Use them above the conference table to drive home only your most important speaking points. Since they can be seen as aggressive, be careful not to aim them at colleagues across a room. Recall from earlier in this chapter the potent *moutza*-like gesture Zoe Cruz showed at Morgan Stanley to shush a colleague. It was not taken lightly, and two months after sticking up her hand at the board meeting, Ms. Cruz was shown the door.

Reading Palms

I have watched convincers use palm-down gestures in literally thousands of situations to strengthen their ideas, opinions, and commands. Here are four examples from my field notes:

- In the boardroom, a chairwoman uses a *down-turned palm* as a gavel to order: "Quiet, please!"

- A mother disciplines her child using *overturned palms* to accent her words.

- A Ghanaian tribal elder gestures forcefully with *beating motions* of his pronated palm to convince Westerners that his wives *do* prefer polygamy.

- An angry CEO warns senior staff, using a stiffened *palm-down hand* to accent his words: "Starting *today*, I will not accept late reports."

Self-touching Gestures

A fidgeter touches her face or body repeatedly as she talks. At a meeting, *self-touching* gestures may inadvertently telegraph anxiety, confusion, and uncertainty. They compete with other hand gestures, and suggest you are insecure about yourself or your ideas. Colleagues react by taking points away. Since you yourself seem unsure, they're less likely to buy into your plan.

Self-touch is the act of stimulating one's own *tactile receptors* for pressure, vibration, heat, cold, smoothness, and pain. Like a polygraph test, self-touching reflects the arousal level of your sympathetic nervous system's *fight-or-flight* response. Without conscious awareness, you touch your body when emotions run high to comfort, relieve, or release pent-up stress.

Since they're so sensitive, lips are favorite places for fingertips to land and deliver their reassuring body contact. Self-stimulating behaviors such as holding an arm or wrist; massaging a hand; and scratching, rubbing, or pinching the skin increase with anxiety and may signal fear or uncertainty.

Primatologists call these behaviors displacement activities because they are triggered by nervous energy. Brought on by conflict, stress, or uncertainty caused by the approach of an unknown newcomer, for example, a chimp may "displace" its nervousness by scratching its head. "The more intense the anxiety or conflict situation, the more vigorous the scratching becomes," Jane Goodall writes. "It typically occurred when the chimpanzees are worried or frightened by my presence or that of a high-ranking chimpanzee" (Lawick-Goodall 1968, 329). Emotionally released scratching has been observed in gorillas, baboons, and patas monkeys in similar contexts.

At the risk of micromanaging, I'd advise that you willfully withhold the urge to scratch while answering your boss's questions at staff meetings, lest you appear uncomfortable or uncertain on the hot seat. As you should not let colleagues see you sweat under pressure, they should not see you fidget under stress. Dr. Goodall's comment about chimps bears repeating: "The more intense the anxiety or conflict situation, the more vigorous the scratching becomes." So don't let the boss catch you scratching.

DECEPTIVE HANDS

As hands convince, they can also deceive. In one of my assignments for a company I need not name, I was asked to collect salary figures for the national office's staff. This was a very sensitive task. The company's board of directors wanted to see how they measured up to industry standards of compensation. In simpler words, were they paying staff too much or too little to do the job?

I visited the company's national trade association and bought the latest compensation survey. A quick look at the salary ranges revealed that the company paid on the low end of the scale. Lower pay was evident for all staff except the executive director and the director of finance, who, the figures indicated, were compensated well above average. Instead of e-mailing my findings, I walked down the hallway for a face-to-face meeting with the company's number-two leader, José, the finance director.

I relayed the news to José and told him it looked like the company was low in its compensation for most staff positions. José met my eyes, inhaled, leaned back in his chair, and gripped the armrests. In a flat monotone voice he answered, "You know, the more money you make, the more you pay out in taxes. If you made more money, you'd pay more taxes, so you'd be no better off. I sometimes wish I made less money so I wouldn't have to pay more myself."

My jaw dropped, but I had the presence of mind to keep my lips closed so I don't think he noticed. It wasn't José's corporate doublespeak that surprised me, but his curiously detached demeanor. A usually excitable man given to leaning forward over his desk and accenting statements with adamant, palm-down gestures, the leaned-back José seemed disengaged, disingenuous, and remote. Moreover, he was gesture-free. Both hands held tightly to the armrests and had nothing to say. From his body language, it was perfectly clear that José was deceiving me. He didn't believe what he himself was saying, so why should I?

In work I did with the FBI Polygraph Program, I learned that reading the body's deception cues can be as revealing—if not more so—than reading squiggles on a lie-detector chart. Should an employee fail a polygraph, the official report will read "D.I.," deception indicated. Judging from José's hands as he explained the discrepancies in pay, I'd give him a D.I.

According to specialists in the body language of deception, people who lie show key behaviors that deviate from truthful responses (Burgoon et al. 1989). Since José almost always spoke with his hands—indeed, used profuse speaking gestures—the act of withholding them suggested deceit. For decades, studies have agreed that fabricators use fewer body and facial movements, and significantly fewer hand movements, during deception compared to truth-telling (Vrij et al. 1997). José's suddenly deadpan face and motionless hands gave him away, and I'd caught him in a lie worth noting in my journal. For watching wildlife there is the Serengeti. But for watching people, the workplace is an anthropologist's dream.

———

Hands—their gestures, shapes, and movements—are great communicators in the office. Wrists, palms, and digits bear your closest attention on the job. In this chapter, we've seen how hands can be used to strengthen or weaken an argument, help or hinder understanding across a tabletop, give or withhold truth at a meeting. In the next chapter we turn our attention to shoulders, frequently overlooked body parts with unusual—and unmistakable—tales to tell.

Nuanced with Shoulders

Whenever I heard "no" on an assignment, I looked to the speaker's shoulders to see if it was a serious refusal or one that might be negotiated.

—David Givens

Few of our body parts are as expressive as shoulders. As you'll learn below, they can carry a number of important messages. Their pitching, lifting, rolling, and flexing movements have a great deal to say about feelings and moods in the workplace—or workstation. On July 11, 1996, while orbiting in the Russian space station Mir, U.S. astronaut Shannon Lucid shrugged her shoulders, tilted her head, and gestured with her palm up as she answered questions about her six-week delay in returning to Earth. "You know," she told NBC's *Today* show, "that's life."

Ms. Lucid's shoulder shrug from her workstation in space showed viewers on Earth how powerless she felt about her predicament. All she could do was wait. There was no anger, anxiety, or fear in her gesture, just uncertainty as to when she would return home, and resignation in the face of her unforeseen delay. Powerlessness, uncertainty, and resignation are core meanings of the shoulder-shrug display as originally described in 1872 by Charles Darwin.

A shrug in the vastness of space means the same as a shrug in the Lilliputian state of Delaware. On the earthly plain, consider the shoulder shrug given on April 12, 2006, in the Delaware State House of Representatives. After hearing arguments from physicians and opposing trial lawyers, the House Economic Development, Banking & Insurance Committee voted 5 to 5 on a motion to release a proposed medical malpractice bill for consideration by the full House. Since a tie vote meant the motion was defeated, committee chair Donna Stone noted the outcome and duly adjourned the meeting.

But as representatives left the room, majority leader Wayne Smith, the bill's sponsor, rushed in to try and save the day. Smith was accompanied by a tardy, last-minute voter—Representative Pam Thornburg—who could break the tie simply by signing on late. According to AP reporter Randall Chase, "Stone shrugged her shoulders and told Smith the meeting was adjourned, but she offered no resistance when Smith told her to let Thornburg sign the bill and allow its release."

Ms. Stone's visible shrug that day had two meanings. First, like astronaut Lucid's shoulder shrug above Earth, Stone's was a nonverbal show of helplessness, of powerlessness to revisit the vote. Second, in the context of her impromptu meeting with the House majority leader, Stone's shrug suggested uncertainty, enough doubt to embolden Smith's push to allow Thornburg her belated vote. Thanks, in part, to a shoulder-shrug cue, the motion passed.

"When a man wishes to show that he cannot do something, or prevent something being done, he often raises with a quick movement both shoulders," Charles Darwin wrote (Darwin 1872, 264). Today, the shoulder shrug is seen as a widespread sign of resignation, uncertainty, and doubt. In business, "Yes, I'm sure" said with lifted shoulders means "I'm not so sure"—as in, "I guess." When Donna Stone said, "The meeting's adjourned," her shoulders added a "maybe."

A nuance is a subtle expression of meaning, feeling, or emotional tone. Lifting, flexing, or pitching the shoulders adds subtle misgivings to words. At the Delaware House meeting, Donna Stone's nuanced shoulders were a case study in the body politics of making a deal.

READING THE SHRUG

In my work as a communications consultant, reading shoulders has enabled me to gauge the seriousness of a client's no. "No" is a usually negative response given to express refusal, denial, disbelief, or disagreement. It is an ancient word that comes from the seven-thousand-year-old Indo-European root *ne,* for "not." An informal term for emphatic negation heard in today's workplace is "no way." More assured than the simple no word, no way is never said with a shrug.

Whenever I heard no on an assignment, I looked to the speaker's shoulders to see if it was a serious refusal or one that might be negotiated. As in Representative Stone's case, when I saw shoulders flex forward or lift, ever so slightly, I knew the no was a maybe.

Since shrugs are fleeting and often hard to see, you need to watch carefully. To shrug is to lift, raise, or flex forward one or both shoulders. The gesture is a widespread sign of emotional uncertainty. Shrug cues may modify, counteract, or contradict verbal remarks. As noted earlier, with the statement "Yes, I'm sure," a lifted shoulder suggests "I'm not so sure."

The shoulder shrug bears an interesting relationship to the English word "just," as in, "I don't know why I took the money—I just took it." In this sense, "just" conveys a feeling of uncertainty as to motive. The word also connotes "merely," as in "Just a scratch." These diminutive aspects of the word resonate with the cringing, crouched aspect of all shoulder-shrug displays.

A shrug from a colleague at a board meeting suggests that that colleague may be minimizing your suggestion or new idea by shrugging off its importance. It can be used by a rival to show others in the room that your contribution has little or no value. The word itself, which comes from Middle English *shruggen* ("get rid of"), suggests smallness, as do other "shr-" prefixed words such as "shrew," "shriek," and "shrimp." "Shr-" words are grammatically marked, "little"-seeming, and often feminine (Givens 1986). Thus, in a meeting a co-worker may belittle your ideas merely by shrugging a shoulder. Though the word is phonesthetically small-sounding, the gesture itself packs a punch.

Detecting a shrug comes in handy when asking about deadlines. Since workplace deadlines lie endlessly on the horizon, it's nice to have a readable cue to suggest that a due date is negotiable. On assignment for a company in Arlington, Virginia, I learned that deadlines were monitored and enforced by their accounting department. When I had trouble meeting my due date, I'd stop by Rhonda's office in accounting and ask, "Could I have a little more time?"

Rhonda usually answered, "No." But if she shrugged her shoulders as she said the no word, I knew I had a chance for an extension. If she kept her shoulders rigid, I took it as a sign the deadline was date certain. As is typical of most nonverbal signals, Rhonda never knew she gave off the cue. Though out of her awareness, Rhonda's shoulders told me how far I could push.

"Whenever I heard 'no' on an assignment, I looked to the speaker's shoulders to see if it might be negotiated."

The company director's shoulder shrugs were readable, too, even when he wore a business suit. The shoulder pads in his suit jacket may have somewhat masked John's movements—Rhonda's were more obvious beneath the soft fabrics she wore—but the boss's shrugs showed nonetheless as his pads slightly rose. "When do you need my report?" I'd ask. "Monday," he'd answer. The tiniest rise meant I had leeway; no shrug meant the deadline was fixed.

Trapezius and *levator scapulae* muscles lift the shoulder blades. The former muscle, assisted by *pectoralis major, pectoralis minor,* and *serratus anterior,* flexes the shoulders forward as well. Shoulders are so emotional because, like the facial muscles of expression, trapezius is controlled by emotionally sensitive special visceral nerves. Whether in the face, the neck, or the back, muscles controlled by special visceral nerves act on impulse. Neither Rhonda nor her boss could will their shoulders to be still.

The shoulder shrug is one of my favorite cues. It always has something revealing to say. In my field notes, I've recorded others' observations of the shoulder-shrug cue along with my own:

- Since they're dramatized in the entertainment industry, shoulder shrugs draw notice and sometimes even commentary. Actor James Dean's defensive shrug is said to have set his style apart from stiffer performances of male leads of his time. The contrast between Dean's nonverbal diffidence and Rock Hudson's square-shouldered dominance in the 1956 movie *Giant,* for example, is so dramatic it seemed shoulders had been written into the script. But they had not, for Dean's shrug, according to *On the Waterfront* (1955) director Elia Kazan, was "natural." Dean shrugged all the time. In the business world— especially if your business is acting—frequent shoulder shrugs make you seem vulnerable. Since being vulnerable can open you up to verbal attack, don't show your shrugs in the boardroom.

• In the sports industry, among professional golf, baseball, basketball, and football players, the shoulder shrug plays a curiously prominent role. Googling the phrase "shrugged his shoulders," for instance, yields a significant number of athlete anecdotes. Before a big game, players typically shrug and tell journalists they "just need to go out there and play hard to win." Should they win, the shrugs given in interviews after the game also show uncertainty, palpable doubt about how they got the job done. As in business generally, there's a great—though largely unacknowledged—element of chance in achieving success.

In few occupations are colleagues as openly honest about the role of chance—of pure luck—in winning as are professional athletes. Even the great ones shrug as they acknowledge, and kowtow to, the odds. On January 25, 1998, in an NBC Sports interview conducted after his team had won Super Bowl XXXII in San Diego, I watched as the Denver Broncos quarterback, John Elway, shrugged his shoulders and said, "I can't believe it." You're unlikely ever to get this level of honesty about luck, chance, and the iffy role of odds from your stockbroker. When your broker picks a winner, his shoulders remain squared, as if confident, beneath the pads of his suit jacket.

• In the often bellicose business of national politics, complete honesty is a rare commodity. Since whatever they say is liable to cost votes, politicians choose words with care. Nonetheless, though hidden within shoulder-padded business jackets, a politician's shoulders can be relied upon to "tell it like it is." The candidate may be skilled in oratory and debate, but his naive and unschooled shoulders will support—or disavow—public pronouncements. In the business world shoulders are usually anatomical loose cannons that say whatever they feel like saying.

In his televised public apology on September 9, 1998, in Orlando, Florida, former U.S. chief executive Bill Clinton shrugged his shoulders as he said, "I've done my best to be your friend. But I also let you down, and I let my family down, and I let this country down." Without any schooling at all, Mr. Clinton's shoulders kowtowed to the public in acknowledgement of his unseemly affair with White House intern Monica Lewinsky. It was an unusual case of congruence between politico-speak and body language. The two are often at odds, but on that September day in Orlando both Mr. Clinton's shoulders and his speech told the truth.

My field notes include observations of ordinary folk as well. Whether you work for Microsoft, Boeing, or GE, after reading this chapter you will notice that your co-workers lift their shoulders the same way children lift theirs. While vocabulary and diction improve with age and education, shoulders remain largely untutored throughout life. They do as they please without remorse or reflection.

- Responding to his father's question—"Do you have your lunch money?"—a son's left shoulder lifts slightly as he answers, "Yes." The father replies, "Better make sure." Answering her boss's query—"Do you have your newsletter column done?"—a manager's right shoulder rises. The boss replies, "Can you finish it up by tomorrow?" Unbeknownst to either the schoolchild or the older-and-wiser manager, shoulders had spoken on their behalf.

- Leaning forward at the waist in a sort of corporate curtsy that lowered his head three inches from standing height, a finance director peeked around his boss's doorway and lifted both shoulders as he asked softly, "May I talk to you, sir?" The director's request was as ingratiating as any I've seen in any workplace, and I added it to my notebook of observations. If the boss's corner office and imposing desk seemed to say, "I am Oz, the great and powerful," the director's shoulders seemed to reply, "I am Dorothy, the small and meek." Lasting less than two seconds, the finance director's kowtow worked and entry was granted.

The Shoulder Shrug

Shoulder shrugging has been seen in our primate cousin the South African baboon as a sign of fear and uncertainty, and as a response set off by the startle reaction (Hall and DeVore 1972). In monkeys, apes, and humans alike the shrugging gesture originates from an ancient, protective crouch mediated by neural pathways designed for bodily bending and flexion withdrawal. The vertebrate crouch display, which has been used for millennia, consists of bending motions designed to remove an animal from danger. A reflexive act controlled by the spinal cord, bending the body moves it away from hazards, shrinks it to reduce exposed surface area, and makes the body visibly "smaller" to see.

Crouching can be traced to an *avoider's response*, which is tactile in origin. So primitive is the crouch posture's flexor (bending) reflex that it's seen even in immature fish and amphibian larvae. Stimulating the skin of these simple creatures causes side-to-side bending movements that, in a watery world, remove them from dangers signaled by the touch.

Similar tactile or "tap" withdrawal movements have been seen in spineless animals, such as the nematode worm. Working through neurons controlling the muscular *stretch reflex*, the worm's body, like ours, automatically bends away from danger. When we shrug, our own shoulders incorporate these ancient defensive crouching motions—derived from the protective tactile-withdrawal reflex—in a gesture for all to see. So incredibly primal is the shrug that we're not aware we do it.

Triggering emotions for shoulder-shrug cues come from our forebrain's amygdala (LeDoux 1995, 1996) and basal ganglia (or "reptilian core"; MacLean 1990). Submissive feelings find expression in coordinated muscle contractions designed to bend, flex, and rotate parts of the skeleton, to "shrink" the body and show a harmless lower profile. Motions of the shrug complex were designed for defense rather than offense, for self-protection in the physical world—as well as for self-protection in the business world we inhabit from nine to five.

The Ultimate Kowtow

We've seen that as a nonverbal signal in office communication, the shoulder shrug is a sign of many meanings, senses, and connotations. Shrugs are highly nuanced, and in face-to-face meetings they can subtly—and in some cases dramatically—change the meaning of spoken words. Like culinary spices, shoulder shrugs can add a hint of doubt, a dash of diffidence, a pinch of dismissal, or a whiff of indifference to vocal dialogue.

The core meaning of the shrug is physical withdrawal—shrinking or crouching away. Seen in the workplace, a shrug shows the body is protecting itself from social exposure. The body will naturally add distance and pull away from people who threaten harm. The finance director who crouched with bowed head in his boss's doorway was protecting against the possibility of dismissal, of not being allowed inside his boss's lair. "I'm busy now," the employer might growl in impatience. So the employee's kowtow begs the boss's pardon beforehand: "Please let me come in, sir." I called it a corporate curtsy, but visibly lowering one's head in a crouch sends the same message whether it's an obedient bow, a curtsy, or a head tilt: "I mean you no harm."

To kowtow is to show a mood of affected deference. Without awareness, our bodies may kowtow when we meet or greet the boss in a hallway, speak up at a staff meeting, or cross paths in the company cafeteria. Shoulders lift, heads tilt sideward, and palms

roll up in deference to bespeak a gestured soft sell. It's neurologi-
cally programmed and happens entirely apart from consciousness.
Don't be surprised, however, should the boss not shrug back. The
great and powerful usually kowtow only to board members, not to
employees downstream.

The word "kowtow" comes from two Mandarin Chinese
words *kòu,* "to knock," and *tóu,* "head." To kowtow is to kneel and
touch your forehead to the ground in submission, respect, or
worship. As with the shrug, the core meaning is to crouch down
and away from danger portended by superior forces on high.
Crouching is the common theme of the kowtow, the Hindu salaam, the Catholic genuflection, and the Islamic prayer posture,
as well as of the corporate shrug in the boardroom. Crouching
down is also the theme of the world's ultimate kowtow: the African *poussi-poussi.*

Poussi-poussi is an extreme form of crouching found among the
Mossi people in Africa's Burkina Faso. Note the duplication of
syllables, which gives a diminutive, "little seeming" sense to the
Mossi word. To perform a *poussi-poussi,* one takes off shoes and
headgear (which add height), sits with the legs tucked to one side,
lowers the body, and beats on the ground (Collett 1983). Eyes
may turn down, palms may turn up, and dust may be thrown on
the head in this, the most self-effacing of all crouch displays. It's
hard to imagine the *poussi-poussi* in a modern office setting, unless
you're watching a colleague grovel for a raise.

A Vocal Shrug

As mentioned earlier, when you ask the boss for a due date on your
next project, listen carefully to her tone of voice. If she says, "Friday" in a deep, Martha Stewart–like voice, then Friday it will be.
You'll see fixed, immobile shoulders along with her authoritative
answer to your question.

But if the boss says, "Friday" in a lighter, Katie Couric voice, you can probably ask for more time. You will likely see flexed or lifted shoulders with this friendlier, softer-voiced answer.

There's good reason for the correlation between shoulder movements and voice tones. Shrugs and vocal softness go together, as do squared shoulders and vocal hardness. The muscles that control the shrug (upper trapezius) and voice quality (tiny muscles of the voice box or larynx) are both governed by the same cranial nerve (cranial XI, a special visceral nerve).

In the office, watch and listen for this congruence between shoulder movements and lighter voice tones. You'll become a better observer of—and listener to—office signals.

A Shrug of Deception

Defined by *The American Heritage Dictionary,* the shoulder shrug is "a gesture of doubt, disdain, or indifference" (Soukhanov 1992, 1673). It is indeed the gesture of many meanings, and here is another: In the business world, a shrug can also be a sign of deception.

Jim managed computer backups from the help desk of a midsize U.S. company. Late one workday a colleague, Opie, stopped by Jim's office to ask him to restore some database backups to the company server. When he asked Opie what had happened to the database files, Jim reported that Opie "shrugged his shoulders, saying that he had somehow corrupted the database and wanted to restore from backup" (Anonymous 2009).

Why would Opie shrug his shoulders at precisely that moment? The word "somehow" would seem to introduce an element of doubt, which could bring on a shrug of uncertainty. However, Jim would soon learn that Opie's shoulder shrug was not a sign of uncertainty but of deception.

Two weeks after Opie's visit to Jim's windowless office, a second colleague, Taj, phoned to ask Jim to back up the same database files to the same server. Then, moments after Jim finished the backup for Taj, the latter called back to ask if Jim had restored the files. When Jim said he'd just done the restore, as per request, there was a "momentary silence" and then, sounding slightly annoyed, Taj indicated he'd found a problem with his database. A face-to-face meeting was imminent. "I'll be right down," Taj said.

"He walked into my office a few minutes later, clearly irate. 'When did Opie ask you to start backing up to this server? It was Opie, right?' I told him that the request had been made a few weeks before. He looked at me for a moment, then spun on his heel and headed back to the developer pen. Sensing something might be about to go down (and that my name could be involved), I followed him," Jim wrote (Anonymous 2009). Clearly, Opie's shoulder shrug was an indication not of doubt (the usual reason for shrugging), but of information withheld. It appeared Opie had something to hide.

A second meeting took place. With an accusing index finger pointed at Opie, Taj told him he knew Opie had been messing with his database. The database in question officially belonged to Taj, and Opie's tampering had caused him to lose all of his file updates. "Opie leaned back in his chair, arms folded," Jim recalled, "and didn't say a word, just rocked in his chair. Taj looked at me, as if for assistance, and I shrugged my shoulders and said, 'I just do the backups'" (Anonymous 2009).

"When a man wishes to show that he cannot do something, or prevent something being done, he often raises with a quick movement both shoulders." Charles Darwin's observation is so prescient I quote it again. Published in 1872, his words describe Jim's behavior to a T. More than a century ago Darwin was the first to sense "helplessness" in the shrugging cue. Jim's shoulder shrug 137 years later sent a clear message that, in his job as backup manager, he was powerless to keep Opie from overwriting Taj's work.

At a fourth face-to-face meeting, the company's IT director met with the three players to settle the dispute. Opie was found guilty of interoffice piracy, of trying to commandeer Taj's project by making bogus backups of his work and copying his own unauthorized work to the server. Opie was not fired for his computer sabotage, but from that point forward he never received a new work assignment from the company.

If Opie's motive for causing digital damage was never fully explained, the meaning of his and of Jim's shoulder shrugs stands out clearly. Though the shrugs looked alike, each had a different meaning. Jim's shrug carried the classic Darwinian sense of powerlessness—"I just do the backups." Opie's signaled deception. Asked why he needed a backup, Opie could not tell the truth, "I need to sabotage my colleague's database." A truthful answer would not serve his purposes, so he had to make one up on the fly: "I somehow corrupted my database" came out instead. Mentally, it's harder to conjure up a lie than to tell the truth. Opie's shoulder shrug showed uncertainty as to the story.

The Sweet Shrug of "Why Not?"

When the rhetorical question "Why not?" is voiced at a meeting, you will often see the speaker's head tilt, palms uplift, and shoulders rise. All three body movements are part of Darwin's larger shoulder-shrug display, which might also include pouted lips, knock-knees (tibial torsion), and pigeon-toes. With "Why not?" the component parts of the shoulder shrug show uncertainty as to motive.

In October 2008 Borders Book Festival director Alistair Moffat summoned courage to invite an esteemed colleague, Dame Joan Bakewell, to participate in his upcoming conference in Melrose, Scotland. The gala event was scheduled for sometime in June 2009. "I asked her if she would be interested in coming to our

festival and, to my delight, she shrugged and said: 'Yes, why not?'"
(Keddie 2009).

Moffat, the businessman, knew Dame Bakewell's name would
help increase attendance and bolster the conference's bottom
line. Asking the prominent UK journalist, TV personality, and
author of *The Centre of the Bed* (2005) would be a gamble. She was a
very important person, a BBC star and the official UK "Voice of
Older People." So he took his chances, made the proposal, and
quickly won her over. His for the asking, she said yes.

"Yes," Dame Bakewell voiced with a shrug, "why not?" But
what made her qualify the yes word with a "why not" and nuance
it with a shoulder shrug? I wasn't present at the meeting between
Moffat and Bakewell, but I'll suggest they may have exchanged a
significant number of *quasi-courting* cues.

"Quasi-courtship" was introduced in 1965 by psychiatrist Al-
bert Scheflen as a term for courtship directed toward nonsexual
ends. The body language of quasi-courtship is similar to that of
the sexual version—animated smiling and laughing, gaze holding, head tilting, head tossing, and, yes, shoulder shrugging—only
it's geared to making business deals, not to making love. In consulting assignments, I frequently see quasi-courtship in offices,
where it's used to build rapport and make the workday more en-
joyable through a metaphor of mock flirtation.

Born in 1933, Dame Joan Bakewell has had a career marked by
public signs of sexuality and allure. She wore very short dresses in
her younger years, had an alleged seven-year affair with a famous
playwright, produced sexually explicit TV shows, and earned
the nickname "the thinking man's crumpet." Based on her professional modus operandi, I'd decode Dame Bakewell's shoulder shrug with Alistair Moffat as a sign of ambiguity as to
motive. Despite their age difference (Moffat was born in 1950),
the excitement of courting was likely present at their 2008
meeting. It was quasi-courtship, of course, not courtship per se,

but I speculate that it may have paved the way for her affirmative answer.

Shoulders in True Office Romance

The line between quasi- and true courtship in the workplace is usually clear. Many of the body-language cues are the same, but they tend to be more exaggerated in the sexual version of courtship. As for shoulders, their messages can be so obviously flirtatious that everyone in the office will notice when a couple is newly smitten. From field notes, I recall watching a man and woman at Starbucks as they flexed, pitched, and rolled their shoulders flirtatiously over lattes. From their shoulders alone, sexual attraction was clear. Should you see these same behaviors in the company cafeteria, you may be witness to a budding office romance.

In *Love Signals* I included a section on "Shoulder Speak":

Shoulders, the paired, jointed girdle connecting arms to the torso, are considered attractive around the world. Their horizontal, angular shape gives the human frame its signature, squared-off silhouette. Rounded deltoid muscles of the upper arms soften the angularity with their curvilinear contour. These conspicuous body parts are singled out for display with shoulder pads that emphasize breadth and with off-the-shoulder blouses and puffy sleeves that feature the deltoids' roundness (Givens 2005, 149).

If shoulder shrugs in the context of business meetings show uncertainty, shrugs in courtship show and suggest yielding. Again from *Love Signals:* "Submissively lifted shoulders invite a partner closer. Seeing the cue reveals one is unlikely to step back, turn away, or brush off the advance. We unconsciously flex and lift our shoulders with those we like" (Givens 2005, 46).

Despite myriad nuanced messages sent and received in the workplace, shoulders rarely appear anywhere in the company handbook. Nor are you likely ever to get training, seminars, or webinars on what they say in the office. As meaningful as any words written in memos and minutes, shoulders betoken emotions, feelings, and moods. Read them carefully to monitor unspoken uncertainty or doubt. When the certitude of words is at odds with a shrug, trust the shoulders. Controlled by older brain centers than those for speaking, shoulder movements are more trustworthy and revealing of mood. They will raise your emotional intelligence in the workplace—if you watch them.

———

In the next chapter, we will move north to decode another surprisingly expressive feature: hair. If your shoulders are usually hidden beneath fabric, your hairstyle is always out there in full public view, broadcasting throughout the workday. Hair is always on display. What does your hair say about you on the job?

Résumé Hair

In the workplace, your hair is your résumé. In the same way that a printed résumé is a brief account of your work history and qualifications, your hairstyle provides a quick visual summary of your status, standing, and role on the job. While your written résumé stays out of sight in a file drawer, your hairdo is prominently on display every working day of your life. If your hands, shoulders, and eyes have tales to tell, your hairstyle—since it's never hidden behind a podium or under a desk—broadcasts continuously throughout the workday. Hair is center stage in the office, enacting your sex, age, qualifications, and peer-group affiliation. Better than a written description, the style, color, shape, and sheen of your hair define you at a glance.

Certainly this is true of the theatrical businessman Donald Trump, whose signature comb-over has been comically described as "unbe-weave-able" and "strangely hypnotic." Trump's hair is "over the top—no pun intended," says Ouidad, owner of the Ouidad Hair Salon in Manhattan. "He's overdone on everything," the stylist said, and added that Donald's cascading locks look like a visor that overpowers his face. Asked what advice she would give, Ouidad said she'd scissor off the long sweep of his bangs and cut the top short (Oldenburg 2004).

Radically trimming the Taj Ma-helmet, however, would so transfigure Mr. Trump's résumé that he'd no longer be "The Donald." Hair is his trademark, so well known that the Donald Trump wig was once a bestselling Halloween costume. Trump's comb-over speaks effectively on his behalf. Though he'd not survive an entry-level job interview with such loud locks—the hair would literally upstage the man—for a businessman of his stature, it creates a bold impression.

So idiosyncratic is hair like Trump's that it violates the first rule of corporate identity: "Be on the same team." With Trump hair you're on your own team standing alone. Until you're the boss, your hairdo is most properly worn as a corporate membership badge. If you work for Microsoft in Redmond, Washington, wear Microsoft hair. If you work for *The Stranger,* an alternative newspaper just across Lake Washington in Seattle, wear *Stranger* hair. Nonverbally, job hair is about fitting in as birds of a feather.

The biggest influence on corporate coifs since 1960 has been the mass media. In the 1960s, antiestablishment shaggy hair for men was made popular by TV images of the Beatles. In the 1970s, very long straight hair for women was popularized by televised images of the American folksinger Joan Baez, whose dark tresses contrasted with shorter, chemical-permanent styles of the time. In the 1980s pop singer Madonna's soft-tousled blond hair popularized a sexier, Marilyn Monroe look of the 1950s. In the 1990s, TV ads of Chicago Bulls player Michael Jordan popularized the shaved-head look once worn by actor Yul Brynner in the 1956 movie *The King and I.* In the 2000s, shaved heads and very short hair have set an alternative standard for men in business.

For women today, the bobbed, highlighted hairstyle of media icon and businesswoman Martha Stewart is a popular standard. Hollywood stylist George Caroll characterizes Stewart's style as simplicity combined with a touch of drama. Martha's business look is shaped in layers from the crown, cut just past the cheekbones, and styled with a side part. By parting on the right-hand side, Stewart adds a touch of Veronica Lake mystique, sweeping the bangs down to partially cover her left eye.

Facial and head hair play a powerful yet curious role in the workplace. It begs the question of why, in the age of Microsoft, Google, and the Internet, hair remains the potent medium of expression it is and will continue to be. The answer, we'll see, is evolutionary, and millions of years older than electronics. As fur-bearing mammals, we have been genetically programmed to search each other's hair for signs of good health, good grooming, and status. Sensitivity to hair in the workplace is mediated by ancient neural circuits wired into our species' old mammalian brain.

What's wrong with big hair in the office? How long should a sideburn be? What do bangs say about competence? What does a beard say about a man's perceived level of credibility? Why is hair so dramatic in the entertainment field and so boring on Wall Street? There are hidden underpinnings in anthropology, biology, and neurology that we can turn to for answers. Just what should your hair say about you on the job?

HAIR FANCY

Fascination with hair has deep biological roots (so to speak) in our mammalian past. In the office we spend an unusual amount of time noticing, monitoring, and commenting on colleagues' head hair, or its absence. This is because we are mammals, fur bearers for whom well-groomed hair is a sign of health and high status. This biological equivalent of scales, feathers, and fur not only keeps our head warm and dry but also protects the braincase from direct sunshine. Hair once provided camouflage to help our ancestors blend into the natural landscape. Today's hairstyles help us blend into the business scene as well.

Hair is made of a tough, insoluble protein called keratin. Scalp hair is an indexical sign that stands for the person upon whose head it grows. Proximity to the face makes head hair a more important index of personality than signs given off by the body's other keratinous organs, such as fingernails and toenails, or the hair on our arms and legs. Eyebrow and eyelash hairs are also indexical signs, but compared to head hair they matter less as signs of identity.

Throughout the world, anthropologists have found perceived magical connections between head hair and the person to whom it belongs. Native cultures from Australia to Zambia believe that possessing a lock of another's hair grants magical power over that individual. In Native North America, Huron, Mohawk, and Iroquois warriors took hair-laden scalps as tokens of the men they'd defeated in war. In the modern world the neatness of hair has become an emblem signifying one's willingness to commit to business on behalf of the firm. Regular haircuts contribute to the team dynamic of discipline.

In 2008 a leading U.S. trading-card firm, Upper Deck Company LLC of Carlsbad, California, began selling plastic-encased strands of hair clipped from such noted historical figures as Abraham Lincoln, Babe Ruth, Jackie Kennedy, and Apache leader Geronimo. Most of the tiny strands came from the authenticated hair collection of handwriting expert John Reznikoff. Posted on eBay in November 2008, a partial link of Mr. Lincoln's hair sold for $24,000. That such a large sum of money changed hands attests to the magic of scalp hair. A nail clipping from one of the sixteenth president's fingers would have earned far less.

Women: Beware the Fanciful Feather

Since the office demands that you appear more serious than you likely are, avoid wearing feathers to work.

"There are certain items which are so girly, so feminine and impractical that you can't help but love them," writes London fashion journalist Samantha O'Neill. "This is true of feathers; they are a frivolous embellishment, they have no purpose except to look superb" (O'Neill 2008).

Feathers form the showy, decorative plumage of birds. Since they're reminiscent of human hair, feathers worn on the job suggest ostentation, much like "big hair." Lovely to look at, but feathers are too fanciful, sensual, and cheeky to wear to work. According to Ms. O'Neill, feathers symbolize a flippant attitude and escapism.

The heyday of feathers in women's fashion came between 1905 and 1914, decades before great numbers of women went to work in offices. This was the historical period of the ostrich-feather craze when women's hats, dresses, and shoes—from New York to Paris—bore plumes of the South African Barbary ostrich (S. Stein 2008). When World War I began in 1914, feathers dropped out of sight as austerity replaced the former frivolity of the day.

Flouncing feathers are delightful to behold and inviting to touch, but they give the wrong message in an office. They can make the most serious woman look and seem like a featherweight.

A Case of Narcissist Hair

Paying thousands of dollars for a strand of hair may seem strange. Yet it's equally odd to pay $1,250 for a haircut. If the strand is an indexical sign of a person, in the workplace the cost of a haircut can be an index of narcissism. Recall from Greek mythology that Narcissus, after spurning the advances of many, including Echo, a nymph, was cursed by Artemis to fall in love with his own reflection in a pool of water. After trying unsuccessfully to get the reflected image to return his love, the young man wasted away and turned into the narcissus flower that bears his name today.

Most of us check the condition of our hair in a mirror before leaving for work, and recheck it in mirrors throughout the workday. This does not make us narcissists. But those who gaze excessively into mirrors do raise the specter of narcissistic personality disorder, or NPD.

Excessive hair primping in front of a mirror was caught on video and shown as an amusing clip on the Internet site YouTube .com in March 2007. In the video John Edwards—then a candidate for the office of U.S. president—repeatedly tousled his bangs in front of a hand mirror to the song "I Feel Pretty." Mr. Edwards's gaze fixed on his hair as he touched, primped, and fiddled with his bangs over and over again, using the tactile pads of his fingertips to tenderly brush the hair back. It was a telling glimpse into how the man truly felt about himself, and a harbinger of seedy things to come in his political career.

Edwards's hair primping was a small sign, but one with major meaning about his hidden vanity and swollen pride. In spoken words on the stump, John Edwards portrayed himself as a champion of the underdog. Yet in deeds he seemed to relish the role of top dog for himself. Excessive preoccupation with how his hair looked may not have signaled full-blown NPD, but it did show that he took his image very seriously indeed. For Mr. Edwards, excessive primping suggested a man who could justify paying not just tens, as underdogs do, but hundreds of dollars for haircuts to project an image of strength.

In a July 2007 interview with *The Washington Post*, John Edwards's Beverly Hills hair stylist, Joseph Torrenueva, revealed that one haircut alone had cost $1,250, which included the cost of Torrenueva's air travel to Atlanta to trim the candidate's locks. "He has nice hair," Mr. Torrenueva said. "I try to make the man handsome, strong, more mature and these are the things, as an expert, that's what we do" (Anonymous C 2007). The article went on to report that the hairdresser charged $300 to $500 for each haircut, plus airfare, hotel, and meals. Since the cost of a man's cut at the time averaged $15, you could say Edwards's concern with his locks at least bordered on narcissism. Some of his colleagues thought he'd crossed the line.

For many who exhibit narcissist signals, the nonverbal tactic is to show positive signs to deflect attention from negatives. In John Edwards's case the pretty-boy hairdo may have masked certain bad-boy tendencies, such as his 2006 love affair with a female campaign employee, a story that was revealed in 2008. Edwards's public admission on August 8, 2008, of behavior unbecoming a presidential candidate was made worse by the fact that John's wife, Elizabeth, has had an ongoing battle with breast cancer. Edwards's unfaithful behavior signaled he was a man not to be trusted. Certainly, the trust factor damaged his chances for a political post in Barack Obama's White House. John Edwards's indexical hair had made a statement that his behavior belied.

In the world of business and politics, hairstyles worn to the office may project patently unreal images. Consider the style of Chinese president Hu Jintao's jet black hair. A photo published in 2007 showed the bespectacled Mr. Hu, then sixty-four, with thick black hair parted on the left and slicked back above his forehead. Since at his age most men show at least a few gray hairs, it's likely that Mr. Hu had opted for the "Chinese solution" to send a barbered image of virility and youth.

In his *Wall Street Journal* article "Chinese Bigwigs Are Quick to Reach for the Hair Color," reporter Jason Leow writes, "Very few of China's political and business leaders these days seem to go gray" (Leow 2007, A1). Leow notes that even Mr. Hu's predecessor, Jiang Zemin, then eighty-one years old, still had coal black hair. In the offices of Chinese business leaders, Mr. Leow remarks, "There is barely a gray hair among the ranks of the richest" (Leow 2007, A24).

In contrast to Chinese bosses, U.S. business and political leaders opt for the "silver solution" to project a message of experience. Gray hair shows they've weathered many storms and know how to lead the way. Gray, moreover, has a precedent in primate evolution. Among our most powerful primate cousins, the mountain gorillas of Equatorial Africa, group leaders are known as silverbacks. As adult males age, the saddle area of their back changes from youthful black to shades of gray, suggesting experience and seniority. Gorilla group members decode the dominant silverback's fur and pay respect to the graying leader. Even if a silverback could dye his saddle black, he'd probably not. The Chinese solution would not be an option in the bush.

As an anthropologist who has observed diverse hair displays in Western offices, I'd make the following points about hair for men and women:

- Wear a hairstyle designed to fit the norms of your industry. The Montana Cattlemen's Association has different standards than the World Bank. You're more likely to find the right look in your industry's trade journal than in the pages of *Esquire* or *Vogue*.

- Use shampoos that accent your hair's natural sheen. Sheen is a sign of health and good grooming. Avoid hair colorings that, while they make you look younger, dull your hair and make you look less fit and able-bodied.

- Don't be too quick to get rid of the gray. Cut in the right style, both for women and men, gray hair lends an air of authority.

Hair Writes a Memo

MEMO

TO: All Colleagues

FROM: A Businesswoman

DATE: Today

RE: What Message My Hair Is Sending

1. **"My bangs say I'm whimsical and fun."** "Indeed, whether wispy and short or soft and long, today's bangs look 'whimsical and fun,' says hairstylist Frédéric Fekkai, who counts Ashley Judd and Sharon Stone among his clients. Even better, notes Cindy Crawford's cutter Stephen Knoll, 'it's a great way for women to disguise frown lines on their foreheads'" (Scott 2000, 129).

2. **"I made a big change in my life."** Women mark lifestyle and career changes with different hairstyles, according to Grant McCracken in his 1996 book, *Big Hair: A Journey into the Transformation of Self.*

3. **"I am confident and outgoing."** A Procter & Gamble study led by Marianne LaFrance of Yale University found that, in the United States, hairstyle plays a significant role in first impressions. For women, short, tousled hair conveys confidence and an outgoing personality, but ranks low in sexuality (LaFrance 2000).

4. **"I'm smart and a fun person."** Medium-length, casual hair suggests intelligence and good nature (LaFrance 2000).

5. **"I'm sexy and rich."** Long, straight, blond hair projects sexuality and affluence (LaFrance 2000).

6. **"I'm attracted to you."** Women may preen and run fingers through their hair around men they are attracted to (Givens 2005).

TO: All Colleagues

FROM: A Businessman

1. **"I'm self-assured, attractive, and narcissistic."** For men, a short, front-flip hairstyle is seen as confident, sexy, and self-centered (LaFrance 2000).

2. **"I am smart and rich, but a bit parochial."** Medium-length, side-parted hair connotes intelligence, affluence, and a narrow mind (LaFrance 2000).

3. **"I'm nice—but sort of careless."** Long hair projects "all brawn and no brains," carelessness, and a good-natured personality (LaFrance 2000).

4. **"I'm the man."** Short, military cuts show off masculine power traits: bony brow ridges, prominent noses, and larger jaws (Givens 2005).

5. **"I'm in serious denial."** According to anthropologists, in many societies shaved heads and short hair symbolize discipline, denial, and conformity (Alford 1996).

Animal Signs

"Hair just keeps on growing," Dr. Mark Miodownik of King's College London writes, "reminding us that our animal nature is constantly bubbling under the surface" (Miodownik 2008). Nowhere is our animal nature more noticeable in the office than on a male colleague's face. Around the world, there has been a growing fashion trend for men in their twenties and thirties to style facial hair into usually neat, clipped mustaches and beards. Today's young men are unleashing the animal for all to see.

Men may project "strength" with dense *facial manes.* Beards optically widen the lower face, while mustaches turn the lip corners downward to project a fiercer look. It is only hair, after all, but to the very visual primate brain, appearances are "real."

Even in Japanese companies, where facial hair traditionally has been frowned upon or banned, young men today arrive at work with facial hair showing. For instance, in 2008 clothing salesman Ken Miura, aged twenty-three, arrived at his store with a shaggy mane of dark-brown hair, a wispy mustache, and a sparse goatee. He would like to grow a thicker beard, he said, "But I'm not hairy enough" (Tabuchi 2008, B10). Mr. Miura is among thousands of Japanese men who now experiment with letting their animal out. Once disallowed, facial hair is becoming an acceptable sign of individuality in the Japanese workplace.

In the United States perhaps half of all male office workers display facial hair. In Iraq mustaches are customarily worn by working men, while in Chinese offices facial hair is notable by its absence. Worldwide, in about two-thirds of societies surveyed by anthropologist Richard Alford, men wear beards and mustaches. Judging from newspaper photos of New York stockbrokers, the men of Wall Street are mostly clean-shaven.

According to Alford, "Because hair also reminds us of our kinship with other animals, hair removal is often explicitly explained as a means of asserting separateness from animals" (Alford 1996, 7). As an anthropologist myself, I find showing more of the hairy side in offices a fascinating trend. It signals a shift from the corporate "We," perhaps most extreme in Japanese companies, to the individual "I" typified in the United States.

As Victor Hugo, author of *The Hunchback of Notre Dame* (1831) noted, animals are the visible phantoms of our souls. Animals are an endless source of inspiration for artists, philosophers, and photographers. They are a major source of companionship, entertainment, symbolism, and food for human beings. The English word "animal" comes from Indo-European *ane-*, derivatives of which include "anima" ("soul") and "animate" ("enliven"). Sending a few good-animal signals to colleagues can energize an office.

Office Bald Guys

We've explored the significance of corporate hair, so let us look now at baldness and the "bald look." The latter has become an increasingly visible statement in the office.

"Hair's a hassle," says Mike Ubl, mission director of the Brotherhood of Bald People (Beck 2008, D1). According to Mr. Ubl, who lost his scalp hair in his early twenties, "All men who lose hair go through a personal journey from denial to acceptance, and ultimately to appreciation. The process can take weeks, months or years, but the experience is the same regardless of the amount of time it takes."

Established in November 2006, the Brotherhood of Bald People's mission is to inspire self-confidence and self-acceptance in the bald community, and to change public perceptions of baldness. Since hair is glorified in media images of models, actors, and rock stars, men who lose hair to male pattern baldness, or MPB, often feel inadequate. Many grieve as MPB steals a defining part of their youthful identity. After experimenting with hair treatments, which rarely work, many men today are shaving their heads.

Though the radical skin-head image sends the wrong message in European soccer stadiums, a shaved head in today's office is a positive sign. It shows that a man has rejected the inadequacy of hair loss in favor of a confident new image. The path from MPB to buzz cut to shaved head takes courage. One must suffer the inevitable office initiation.

On his first day back to work after shaving his head, a man wrote on the Brotherhood Web site, "I had four comments": (1) after an uncontrollable laugh from a co-worker: "It's not because it looks bad, it actually looks good . . . but holy smokes, man, warn me next time!"; (2) from a co-worker in the elevator: "Oh my

God, you have no hair!"; (3) from a co-worker in the restroom: "What happened? Lose a bet?"; and (4) from a boss in the hallway: "What made you do this?" (Que 2008)

After shaving and surviving the initiation phase, most men report that they, their spouses, and coworkers like the new look. Increasingly in the office, the bald look is a sign of the times.

———

Clearly hair, or its absence, sends a continuous message in the office. Unlike shoes that hide under desks, hands that fold beneath tabletops, or eyes that turn away, your hairdo is always on display. Your hairstyle is a nonverbal *signature display* representing who, what, even "why" you are. For human beings, head hair is a badge of identity reflecting membership in a group, and also showing a desire to identify with and be like other people. Rather like a baseball cap, our hair may be used to show we belong on the company team.

As we use our clever human brain to master the latest in information and communication technology (ICT) on the job, our older primate brain takes the measure of our colleagues' hair. ICT addresses parts of our brain's evolutionary new wing, called the *neocortex,* while head hair addresses a more ancient brain area known as the *cingulate gyrus.* The former can learn a computer application; the latter can spot a hair out of place across a boardroom. To make the right impression, you must address your colleagues' newer human and older primate brain at the same time. Good ideas matter in the workplace, but so does hair.

In the next chapter we will turn our attention away from eyes, hands, and hairdos to what we wear to work. In the office, minor details of dress can have major meanings.

SEVEN

Cracking the Dress Code

I can never bring you to realize the importance of
sleeves, the suggestiveness of thumbnails, or the great
issues that may hang from a bootlace.

—Sherlock Holmes to Watson, "A Case of Identity"

In the office, clothing can make or break your persona. "Persona"
is the role your outer self plays at work, as opposed to what you
reveal about your inner self after hours. Since clothing defines
your corporate image, you should dress strategically. As primates,
human beings have a critical eye for details that reflect status, personal grooming, and health. A tiny spot on a tie, a frayed collar, a
glimpse of a wrinkled sleeve—each will be read as an identity cue.
Seemingly minor details can play a major role in defining who you
are on the job. In today's workplace, you are what you wear.

"It feels natural," Philip O'Neill said when asked why he wears
suits and ties to work. On October 13, 2005, O'Neill, an advertis-
ing executive, was named New Zealand's Best Dressed Businessman. While many in his office wore jeans and T-shirts, O'Neill
wore pressed slacks and tailored jackets to stand out from the
crowd. Judges in the best-dressed competition liked his outfits'
"traditional formality combined with a young man's flair."

"First impressions do count," a judge noted, "but standards
need to be maintained week in, week out." On March 7, 2006,

five months after accepting his best-dressed award in New Zealand, Philip O'Neill received a promotion and transfer to a higher-paid position in Melbourne, Australia. Sartorial signals helped speak favorably on his behalf (National Business Review 2005).

· One of Philip O'Neill's favorite outfits, purchased in London, is a gray Dunhill single-breasted suit with pale blue pinstripes. Gray is a serious color that says, "I'll get the job done." Simultaneously, pale blue says, "I'm friendly." Dignity, tenderness, and truth are among the traditional symbolic meanings of the color blue, while for gray, ever since Sloan Wilson's classic novel *The Man in the Gray Flannel Suit* (1955), the color's symbolism alludes to the search for meaning in a world dominated by Western materialism and big business. O'Neill's suit clearly has a lot to say.

Among its hidden messages, the cut of one's suit jacket encodes signs of vital animal strength. To help you loom large in the office, power cues from the mammalian *broadside display* are tailored into every Perry Ellis, Brooks Brothers, and Dunhill suit. Stitched-in pads square the shoulders to exaggerate the size and strength of one's upright torso. Reaching fingertip level, the jacket's hemline visually enlarges a businessman's upper body to apelike proportions. Lapels flare up and outward to enhance the illusion of upper-body strength in a message even a gorilla would understand.

So convincing are size illusions that, around the world, suits have become the premier power outfits for business, politics, and military affairs, both for men and for women. Those padded shoulders not only create the appearance of greater stature, they also mask the inadvertent shoulder shrugs mentioned in chapter 5, which can demonstrate uncertainty in boardrooms and on battlefields alike. Born of togas (200 B.C.), doublets (1300s), short coats (1600s), and court coats (1700s), today's business suit is the evolutionary correct dress for a corporate primate.

Women's business garb took a more feminine evolutionary path. By the 1800s women in the workplace were wearing the likes of lace, feathers, ruffles, corsets, thick undergarments, thickly padded shoulders, and voluminous bustles. It all changed in the 1920s when pioneering French fashion designer Coco Chanel (1883–1971), introduced tailored business suits for women. Inspired by the prevalent menswear image of the day, Chanel jackets featured the same flared-lapel, squared-shoulders look.

The androgyny and power cues Coco Chanel introduced into women's clothing were accompanied by new attitudes of female independence, reflected in women's getting shorter haircuts, smoking in public, drinking cocktails in bars, driving automobiles, and pursuing careers in business. The Chanel suit captured the mood of a dawning age for women in the workplace. Strength had triumphed over fluff and ostentation. To survive in a man's world, women's apparel became more manlike—but thanks to Chanel, still elegant.

A Warning Suit for Men

You may remember Gordon Gekko, the acquisitive character Michael Douglas played in the 1987 movie *Wall Street*. Gekko wore greasy, slicked-back hair; double-breasted suit jackets; deep-pleated trousers; colorful dress shirts with high-contrast white collars; loud, wide neckties; and thick suspenders with showy braces. Mr. Gekko's clothing overstated his presence in the office by drawing eyes to the all-powerful "Me!"

Gordon Gekko was modeled on a real person, Ivan F. Boesky, the bad boy of Wall Street who became infamous for his remarks to business school graduates in 1986: "I think greed is healthy. You can be greedy and still feel good about yourself." Boesky favored black three-piece suits that brought attention to himself and his larger-than-life greed.

Bigger than life was a theme of men's business attire in the early 1980s, when blind ambition reigned on Wall Street and power ruled the day. Bodies were made to look bigger with draping fabric and wide double-breasted lapels, which added weight and authority to ordinary frames. Ivan Boesky himself was a rather frail-looking man in the 1980s, but in the office his three-piece suits made him loom terribly large.

"It was a peacock moment," clothing designer Patrik Ervell says of the cocky 1980s, "when America was really brash" (Smith 2008, D8). Biologists have a term for such ostentation, calling it *aposematic*.

Aposematic bold colors and stark contrasts—like those worn by yellow jackets, bees, and wasps—say, "See me! Beware!" Though men's fashions have toned down considerably since the eighties, aposematic styles—like U.S. designer Tom Ford's boldly striped, double-breasted suits—were once again on display in the spring of 2009.

The "danger look" of 1980s apparel for businessmen will likely be seen in offices, at least sporadically, for decades to come. Like the imperial "me," larger-than-life clothing will never go completely out of fashion.

"I feel that I have a responsibility to project the right image," Karen Firestone of Boston's Aureus Asset Management told *The Wall Street Journal* (Binkley 2007, D8). On March 26, 2007, the Aureus Web site featured a photograph of Ms. Firestone, company president, sitting beside partner Thaddeus Davis, who was wearing a dress shirt and knotted tie without the formality of a jacket.

In the Web portrait, the nonverbal advantage goes to Ms. Firestone in her Luciano Barbera power suit, which clearly signals, "I'm the boss." While Mr. Davis was ready to roll up his shirtsleeves and get down to work, Firestone was ready to lead. What their clothing says is more significant than you might imagine. Even minor details of your own outfits carry major meanings in the conference room.

Responsible for investments totaling $250 million, Karen Firestone, a Harvard Business School graduate, wears Italian-designed jackets from Dolce & Gabbana, Missoni, and Piazza Sempione to look "hip in a sophisticated way." Though she stops short of décolletage, Ms. Firestone isn't afraid to bare her throat and reveal her collarbones to look feminine on the job. Even the way you cover or uncover the vulnerable front of the neck can help or hinder your presentation of self. Throat-baring, a visible sign of diffidence, has been studied in mammals (in dogs and wolves) and in reptiles (alligators and crocodiles). In human beings, the prominence of the "neck dimple," the fleshy indentation below the Adam's apple, has led to diverse fashion statements for exhibiting, adorning, or concealing it from view. (For more on this, see "Baring Your Throat," page 104.)

A VIP Suit for Ladies

Christina Binkley, fashion columnist for *The Wall Street Journal*, loves her St. John Angelina suit jacket and matching skirt. She found that people treated her better when she wore the St. John than when she wore business clothes from Banana Republic or Saks.

"At the office," Ms. Binkley wrote in her "On Style" column, "a colleague complimented my suit and asked, 'Did it cost $1,000?'" (Binkley 2008b, D8). The more she wore it, the more she realized her dark St. John knit gave her a leg up, not only in business but in other areas of life like shopping, dining, and travel.

When she wore her St. John jacket and knee-length skirt, store clerks paid more attention, waiters seated her at high-status tables, and a fellow JFK traveler even carried her bag down the Jetway to her plane. "Is it my imagination," Binkley wrote, "or do New York cab drivers pick me and my St. John over other hailers during rush hour?"

Manufactured by St. John Knits Inc. in Irvine, California, business suits like the ones Christina Binkley wears don't come cheap. They are an investment in a traditionally elegant style that, at a glance, can elevate your status in and outside of the office. The fit, smoothness, and appealing texture of wool-blend fabrics speak volumes about worth on the job. If you take yourself seriously, others will, too.

Prior to collars, shirts, and skirts, there was the unadorned primate body: eyes, teeth, skin, hair, and nails, along with shapes formed of muscle, fat, and bone. Before adornment, our remote ancestors expressed feelings and attitudes in body movements, facial expressions, and postures. With the advent of clothing, the body's nonverbal vocabulary grew. Through the deceptions of fashion, shoulders widened, biceps thickened, and waists thinned. In today's office, your body is what you wear. Do you shop at Banana Republic, Armani, or Nordstrom, and what is your choice communicating at work?

No Detail Too Small

How observant are co-workers of tiny details in your wardrobe? The answer is *very* observant, and female office mates are the most observant of all. For women, paying attention to clothing details begins in early childhood.

When the line of pouty, plump-lipped Bratz dolls became available in U.S. stores in 2001, for example, they were an instant hit. Little girls across the country loved the dolls' edgy clothing, saucy attitudes, and individuality. As sales of the dolls started to fall in 2008, toymaker MGA Entertainment Inc.'s CEO Isaac Larian admitted that his company had "lost focus on what our brand was" (Casey 2008, B1).

Over time, MGA had inadvertently standardized the tiny Bratz dolls' clothing and accessories.

Instead of carrying different handbags, for instance, some of the dolls carried identical plastic bags that looked as though they'd come from the same cookie-cutter mold. To achieve the doll's original appeal of individuality, MGA replaced the look-alike plastic bags with tiny handbags made of cloth bearing different designs. Furthermore, to correct for the too-standardized, plain-jean outfits, MGA embroidered different-color patterns on them to play up the dolls' personality.

While these small details in dress and accessories may seem minor, they made a major difference in how the Bratz dolls were perceived. Little girls took notice. "What attracted them to these [redesigned] dolls was the clothing that was different from one doll to another," said Mr. Larian (Casey 2008, B2). When these youngsters grow up and enter the workplace, they'll no doubt be attuned to office wear with the same focused eye.

WATCH WHAT YOU WEAR

Since deadlines are omnipresent in the workplace, it's important that you wear a wristwatch. Seeing a wristwatch on your arm is a reassuring sign to your boss that you really do care about time. Though you can tell time on a computer, on your cell phone, or on the company wall clock, none of these venues shows your personal commitment to meeting deadlines as visibly as the timepiece strapped to your wrist.

How you tell time in the office also speaks about your age. Co-workers from Generation Y—the Millennials born after 1982—may not wear wristwatches. Many in this cohort get the time from laptops, iPods, and cell phones instead. Nonetheless, Millennials should wear at least a token wristwatch to reassure an older boss that time is important to them. A good bet would be Fossil's Analog Black Dial, an inexpensive, fashionable token of belonging to Generation Y. The message of this trendy watch, in fact, is more about belonging to the group than about caring for time.

Born between 1961 and 1981, Generation X workers often wear large, very visible sporting watches that are water resistant to one hundred meters. The size and broad face of a sports watch show an aggressive commitment to meeting office deadlines (along with an unspoken desire to be out of the office snorkeling, hiking, or on safari). A dress shirt's cuff size may even need to be widened to make room for the thick action watch.

Your office's baby boomers, who were born between 1943 and 1960, may also wear Generation X sports watches. Doing so sends a youthful message. Most boomers, however, wear sleeker, more elegant watches of platinum or gold to display accumulated worldly success. If your boss wears a high-end success watch like Cartier's Ballon Bleu, you should definitely keep a timepiece strapped to your wrist, and roll up your sleeves. The Cartier clearly says, "Time is money."

How important are wristwatches in the corporate world? Judging from display ads in *The Wall Street Journal*, very important. In the October 3, 2008, edition, for example, there are sizeable ads for Carl F. Bucherer ("Fine Swiss Watchmaking"), Audemars Piguet ("*Le maître de l'horlogerie depuis 1875*" [Master of watchmaking since 1875]), and Ulysse Nardin's ("Since 1846") Maxi Marine Diver. In 1899 sociologist Thorstein Veblen popularized the notion of "conspicuous consumption" in his classic volume, *The Theory of the Leisure Class*. Veblen showed that rich and poor alike try to impress others with the objects they conspicuously display. In the office, wristwatches are about more than keeping time. They show conspicuous care about time itself.

Are You Red or Blue?

The badge you wear in the office may reveal more than your name and department. It may also reveal your personality type.

At Acxiom Corporation, a global marketing firm based in Little Rock, Arkansas, everyone wears a color-coded badge. If your badge is red, you're a "problem solver." If it's green, you're a "communicator"; yellow, a "detailed scheduler"; or blue, a "planner" (Gutner 2008, D4). These are the four personality labels—for all to see—assigned after each employee takes the forty-five-minute, 298-question Birkman Method personality test.

Dana Lund, a manager at Acxiom, took the test and learned she was a planner. Knowing she was "blue" helped Ms. Lund deal with others of both the same and different colors in her office. "It has helped me to learn how to interact better with work teams," she said, "and to leverage my strengths in the workplace" (Gutner 2008, D4).

Founded in 1969 in Conway, Arkansas, Acxiom had offices in twelve countries around the world in 2008. The company updates 10 billion data records monthly, according to its Web site, and conducts 125,000 background checks each month. As an anthropologist, I find it strange that while Acxiom deals in billions of data sets, management lumps its employees into one of merely four categories. If human beings are more complex than chimpanzees, you wouldn't guess it from Acxiom badges.

Those color-coded name badges say more about Acxiom than about its employees. According to Annie M. Paul, author of The Cult of Personality (2004), the psychology tests a company uses are more for the convenience of the employer. "It's not about helping someone understand themselves really or explore facets of their personality," she says. "It's really about putting that person in a box and putting a label on them to make the workplace work more smoothly, or to make hiring go more quickly" (Manthey 2008). As for the color-coded badges, what you wear is not necessarily who you are.

ABOVE THE WAIST

Start with Your Shoulders

For a more powerful look in the office, begin with your shoulders. How you clothe them sends a primate-inspired message about strength or weakness. Squared, widened shoulders are visibly "strong," while rounded, drooping, or slumped shoulders are "weak." In monkeys, apes, and human beings, the message is the same. What you wear on your shoulders to the office each day can make you seem like a player or a pushover.

Recall Philip O'Neill's Dunhill suit and the power built into its jacket. The suggestion of simian strength is a message both men and women can send to assert presence in the office. You may remember the broad-shouldered look women adopted for office wear in the 1980s. Women entered the workforce in droves, and the message of their jackets' major broad shoulders—"I am woman, hear me roar"—was impressive. But the jackets turned out to be too strong, too brawny for comfort, and, like dinosaurs, big-padded shoulders went extinct.

Yet the principle of showing an enlarged upper body on the job has survived. A subtler broadening of the shoulder area can hint at power without overstating the claim. For women, the ideal is to combine authoritative shoulders with femininity, comfort, and style. For men, the ideal is to wear authority-connoting shoulders, but without the ostentation of a gangster suit. Suggestions of strength work better than blatant power displays.

Baring Your Throat

In formal office settings, such as meetings of the board of directors, participants arrive with their necks covered. You see knotted ties, silk scarves, button-up collars, and chokers covering the front of the neck. Notice that such coverings mask the fleshy, hollow indentation below the Adam's apple called the *throat dimple*. Revealed by our upright posture and hairless skin, the throat or neck dimple is one of the more vulnerable parts of the body, with little but skin protecting the windpipe. The suprasternal notch, as physicians call the dimple, is the area through which incisions are made to perform a tracheotomy.

An article that I contributed to in the British journal *New Scientist* frames it like this: "The idea that body language taps into non-conscious thought is not a new one. It has spawned generations of self-help books on how to succeed in interviews, or read the signs that your boss fancies you. Consider the indentation at the base of the neck . . . Revealing it is a universal sign of submission and approachability in all mammals and a courtship cue in humans. So a man who loosens his tie in the presence of a potential mate may unwittingly be expressing his attraction" (Spinney 2000).

A visible sign of submission, throat baring has been studied in dogs, wolves, and crocodiles. The prominence of our own rather thin necks as we face each other and speak has led to diverse cultural fashions for exhibiting, adorning, or covering the throat's frail dimple. As in skirt length, neckwear varies with changes in the business cycle, opening up when times are good, and closing—as if for protection—when times are bad.

Dress Down Demise

When business goes down, shirt collars button up. Due to an economic slowdown in mid-2001, Jim Kresse of Tacoma, Washington's *News Tribune* duly noted, "On Wall Street and points west, much of corporate America is again buttoning the top button and leaving the khakis at home" (Kresse 2001, D3).

*An exposed throat dimple
suggests openness.*

In battle, anthropologists have learned, even shirtless men cover their throats. The costume of the African Masai warrior, for example, which consists of a red tunic worn over bared shoulders and arms, includes a layer of beaded necklaces to mask the neck. In the corporate world's less physical but more verbose combative arenas, an executive's silk tie or MBA scarf plays a similar role.

"The most common [business scarf]," writes Susan Bixler, author of *The Professional Image,* "is the *front tie bow*; it adds softness and femininity and is almost universally flattering. It is easy to wear and looks very good with a suit. The scarf should be attached to the blouse in the back so it will stay in place" (Bixler 1984, 169). "A scarf," fashion expert Véronique Vienne adds, "should always be tied in a hurry. Perfect symmetry makes it look dowdy" (Vienne 1997, 158).

The earliest necktie-like garment for men may have been the neckband worn by Roman legionnaires. Later, in the French Revolution, neckbands signified political stances. The color white stood for conservative or "conventional," and black for "revolutionary." Later still, the nineteenth-century cravat survived as a precursor to the modern-day tie, as a means to show moods, occupations, and allegiances—and to cover bared throats around a conference table. For women in the 1890s, according to the American literary critic

Elaine Showalter, the black necktie became the feminist uniform of the "New Woman" (Showalter 2001).

Male or female, the human neck itself is rather slim and suggestive of vulnerability. Thus, a man may "widen" his neck with a button-up shirt collar and knotted tie. The best knot, Susan Bixler advises, is the standard four-in-hand slipknot. If you want to be an eccentric or a standout nonconformist, wear a bow tie. It covers the throat but does little to enhance your image. In contrast, a longer necktie adds an eye-catching vertical line to accent the ascending height of your face, head, and torso. Wearing a standard tie makes you stand up "straighter" and look "taller." Moreover, your dress shirt's right and left collar points visually juxtapose to suggest an "arrow" shape that points upward, drawing eyes to your face.

In an interview with John Tierney of *The New York Times,* we talked at length of neckties, business, and bared throats. I predicted that the more we transition to an information economy,

Wearing a tie makes you stand up "straighter" and look "taller."

the less we'll need to cover our throats. When an employee knows more about the company software than the boss does, the latter's absolute power wanes. As John later wrote in his column, "That's why the necks can now be bared, said David B. Givens, the anthropologist who coined the term 'neck dimple.' 'The exposed-neck look in business attire is a true paradigm shift,' Dr. Givens said. 'In the old days of just a few years ago, you had to look powerful in business. But now information has won out over brute politics and corporate hierarchy. The information-rich young staff gained power and pushed for casual dress, and the first items removed were the MBA scarf and the necktie. When you've been to Information Mecca, you no longer need to wear the veil. It's redundant as a power cue'" (Tierney 2000).

Dressing Down Lord Winston

Lord Winston used to show up in the offices of Wine Enthusiast Cos., a wine accessories company based in Mount Kisco, New York, dressed in a jacket, sporting an ascot, and carrying a glass of red wine. If the lord looked uppity and standoffish, it was due to his ascot, and to the peculiar stance he adopted with his wineglass. Lord Winston's bald forehead tipped precipitously downward, with his nose angled close to the glass to savor the smell of his vintage. Immersed in his olfactory world, he gave co-workers the impression they hardly mattered. All that mattered was the wine.

As he sniffed the wine's bouquet, Lord Winston's ascot sent a message of superiority and disdain. An ascot is a formal necktie that flares out widely in front, more expansively than a standard business tie. In the early twentieth century, a plain gray ascot was worn for business. Today's ascot is made from very thin silk with colorful printed designs. Wearing an ascot to the office can mark you as a snobby member of the upper class, or worse, as a fanciful playboy.

Lord Winston is not a real person, of course, but a cartoon logo.

Created in 1979, he's the Wine Enthusiast company's iconic, if stuffy, trademark. When the company decided to make its products—wineglasses, corkscrews, and specialty refrigerators—more appealing to customers who were not necessarily wine connoiseurs, management deemed Sir Winston should become more approachable and less of a snob.

To refresh its logo, the company revoked Winston's lordly title, removed his ascot, and changed his stance. Today the cartoon figure, known simply as Winston, wears an open collar and lifts his wineglass above his nose in a friendly toast. "He's redesigned to be more approachable," said Gregg Lipman of the CBX company in New York, the firm that helped Wine Enthusiast make Lord Winston friendlier on the job (Covel 2008). Minor tweaks to stance and, importantly, removal of neckwear made a major difference for the brand.

COUNTERSUIT SIGNS

In the way he dresses for work at the office, Trevor Kaufman is a corporate iconoclast. An iconoclast is one who overthrows traditional ideas or practices. Mr. Kaufman, who is CEO of Schematic, a digital branding agency with offices in the United States and London, England, has overthrown the traditional practice of wearing a suit. On August 7, 2008, Kaufman, thirty-eight, was quoted as saying, "A suit has become something you wear when you're asking for money" (Binkley 2008a, D1).

According to *Wall Street Journal* fashion writer Christina Binkley, a business suit today can signal old-fashioned inflexibility. Wearing one in a creative high-tech, sports, or entertainment field can be a liability.

The message Trevor Kaufman sends in his corporate clothing is one of relaxed authority, known as "CEO casual." Kaufman conducts business in blue jeans, for example, with brown Prada loafers, a white dress shirt with opened collar and rolled-up sleeves, and a thick Audemars Piguet wristwatch. How can such a casual work outfit lend authority to the human frame? The secret is in the details.

Mr. Kaufman makes sure his dark blue Levi's 511 jeans are professionally pressed. His tailored shirts are pressed as well, nearly wrinkle-free, and his expensive shoes are highly polished. You will never see a collar point tilted up or bent out of alignment. That the collar itself is open at the throat shows vulnerability, balanced by the strength of Kaufman's sinewy wrists. These are the details that connote casual authority in the office. These are the details that say, "I needn't wear a suit."

It's hard to overstate the premise that, in the office, you are what you wear. Seemingly minor details of dress and adornment have major consequences in how you're perceived on the job. In the next chapter, we explore the unwritten rules of shoes. Major carriers of personality, shoes may sit low on your body, but they speak loudly of your position, power, and standing in the firm.

EIGHT

The Souls of Business Shoes

Shoes hold the key to human identity.
—Sonja Bata, Founder of the Bata Shoe Museum in Toronto
(Trueheart 1995, C10)

Magazine, newspaper, and Web-site articles are replete with advice on the best ways to succeed in job interviews. Many interview tips are nonverbal in nature and recommend, for example, that you smile, give a firm handshake, and return eye contact. Underscoring the importance of feet in the job interview, there are more than a few suggestions pertaining to shoes. While shoes cannot speak, they are noticed, and their nonverbal messages are loud and clear.

"Wear lace-up, leather business shoes," men are advised, "shined, and preferably black." "Don't wear shoes with worn heels." "Don't wear cowboy boots, even in Texas." "Don't wear Nikes, Keds, or Crocs." "Wear matching, dark-colored—never white—socks."

It's impressive how much footwear matters in job interviews, which are supposedly more about competence than feet. And women are given advice as well: "Don't wear heels that are too high," they are told, "or too clunky." "Don't wear sandals or flip-flops." "Don't wear flats." "Don't wear overly colorful red, yellow, or blue shoes." "Don't wear submissively pink hues." "Do wear hosiery." Above all, "Don't show your toes."

"I don't want to see someone with bare legs and open-toed shoes giving me the news," a complainer on AOL writes. "Why can't Katie Couric look professional?" (Simonidou 2007).

The best shoes for business, the complainer might agree, would be serious shoes. In the beginning of her job as *CBS Evening News* anchor, Katie's peep-toe shoes belied the seriousness of her reports. Revealed toes gave off patently sexual messages that clashed with the gravity of world events. Nobody likes a prude, but a little prudishness in footwear is required on the job. Concealing your feet in closed-toe shoes projects a fashionably formal image with the unspoken message: "Take me seriously—I mean business."

Heels and soles send messages, too. For men and women alike, the bottom-line choice in business footwear is between shoes that stand you up on tiptoes, or shoes that anchor your feet firmly to the ground. Visually, high heels suggest that a woman's feet are destabilized. Her body weight seems to defy earth's gravity as she rises above the terrestrial plain. By contrast, men's oxfords anchor a man and solidly tether his feet to terra firma. Your best business shoe is a compromise between high heels and brogues to show you are down to earth but not completely inflexible.

A high-end business shoe for women is Bruno Magli's "Jolyn," a sleek, two-and-a-half-inch-heel, pointy-toed pump. "The perfect fit, they are so comfortable—and I've received lots of compliments," a woman wrote of her Jolyns (Virginia 2007). Like other pumps, Jolyns slim the foot, reveal the instep, and showcase the feminine ankle. Their sex appeal is inherent, but also not as blatant as Couric's open-toed look.

The slimness of pumps evolved from a narrow shoe called the

poulaine, originally from Poland, which was popular with men in the fifteenth century. So long was the tip of its tapering toe—and so suggestive when wagged back and forth—that in 1468 the pope condemned the poulaine as "a scoffing against God." The poulaine died out, but the message of its timid taper lives on in Bruno Magli pumps, which suggest, "I'd rather charm than stomp you."

In business a decent stomping shoe for men is Banana Republic's "Positano," a wide, blunt-toed dress oxford. The Positano broadens a man's feet, while its thick sole and hard heels threaten to trample any who get in his way. Like other oxfords, the Positano is a dominant style of footwear not unlike thick-soled "beetle crushers" of the 1950s, crepe-soled desert boots of the 1960s, and aggressive Dr. Martens of the 1990s. Though invisible beneath boardroom tables, shoes are the first thing people notice when you come to the office, and the last thing they see when you leave.

Dominant business shoes are robust—wide, thick, and heavy—to accent the size of the foot and its ability to stomp. For historical context, the oldest stomping shoes are sandals from ancient Egypt with pictures of enemies painted on their soles. More recently in the Middle East, you may recall April 9, 2003, video images of Baghdad men stomping on the toppled statue of Iraq's late dictator, Saddam Hussein. As a symbolic act, hitting the fallen figure with heels is not unlike a sumo wrestler's ceremonial stomp in the ring. Both are postural displays that demonstrate stability, strength, and standing on the earthly plain.

Office Heels

Like skirt length, the height of business-shoe heels rises and falls over time. In his classic study of skirt length, anthropologist Alfred Kroeber found that when stock prices lower, hemlines fall. Likewise, as profits plummeted and worldwide recession loomed in fiscal

2008, heel heights rose. Both skirt length and heel size reflect the volatile emotions associated with business cycles.

The dismal week ending October 10, 2008, was one of the worst ever recorded for the U.S. stock market. In 2008 designer Manolo Blahnik added a record-setting six-inch heel to his shoe line for women. Though new to the market, the six-inch style accounted for 30 percent of Blahnik's shoe business that year. Meanwhile, other designers—including Yves Saint Laurent, Marni, and Christian Louboutin—added super-size heels and platforms to their own fall lines.

Overall, autumn 2008 saw a markedly taller trend in heel height from the previous three to four inches of 2007 and earlier years. Not surprisingly, podiatrists noted increases in foot and ankle injuries as a result of wearing tall shoes. Los Angeles foot doctor Joshua Kaye said, "It's like you're walking on stilts." Body weight shifts away from boney support to being supported instead by fragile soft tissues and ligaments (Agins 2008, A1). For many women the result is pain.

Yet despite the pain and danger of falling (professional runway models repeatedly stumbled and fell in fashion shows that year) businesswomen continued to wear very high heels to important meetings at work. "I look taller, my legs look longer, and I feel more slender," said Claudia Chen, thirty-three, an event-management business owner in New York (Agins 2008, A16). Ms. Chen wears four-to-five-inch heels despite blaming them for her back problems. "There is a price to pay for beauty," Chen said. High heels will be worn and seen in the office for a long time to come.

SHOES TELL YOUR STORY

Shoes make important statements in the office. So critical are shoes for a proper business image that major newspapers like *The Wall Street Journal* feature them prominently on their front section's second page. Judging from ads in the *Journal*'s October 14, 2008, edition, men's loafers were in style in the fall of that year. The shoes are sleek, clean, shiny—and expensive. Wearing them suggests that you, too, are sleek, clean, well groomed, and seriously invested in your corporate image.

The Allen Edmonds shoe on page A2 (its registered trademark: "Leave an Impression") is shown on a right foot energetically walking forward and leaving a printed impression on the sidewalk that reads, "Owns half of downtown . . . doesn't charge the children's theater rent." Wearing an Edmonds, then, sends a message that you're high-powered but also good to the little people.

As in many footwear ads, the shiny Alden shoe on page A4 is stretched out on the floor, empty, as if awaiting your foot. Alden's mottoes are "Handsewn Perfection" and "Custom Bootmakers Since 1884." The shoe's message alludes to a well-off traditional guy, a man who practices an old-fashioned brand of business. Moccasinlike top-stitching around the toe adds an air of informality.

On A6 we see Belgian Shoes' tiny, understated ad, without trademark or motto. The shoe is left alone to speak for itself. As in previous ads a single shoe does the talking, but from a curious position. The Belgian stands upright on its toe, completely vertical, and floats weightlessly a few inches above the floor. Though it looks like an ordinary loafer, the Belgian shoe is aimed at businessmen who dare to be different, men who eschew the pedestrian low road. A tassel on the toe box accents its contrarian theme.

In the office, each of these shoes tells a story. Since people notice, make sure you choose the one that best tells yours.

A Shoe That Shouts

A popular stomping shoe for women in the office is the (acoustical) pump that's more heard than seen. Its staccato clomping noise can be heard on every uncarpeted hallway. The message is loud and clear: "I am here!" As an anonymous Web posting grumbled: "I just think people who deliberately wear loud heels are saying, 'look at me—notice me—kitty wants some attention!' I can't stand it!" (Anonymous 2007a). The stompers in question are women who wear percussive pumps. These are the shoes that refuse to be ignored or to take no for an answer—these are the shoes that shout.

I'll Wear High Heels If It Kills Me!

Journalist Andrée Aelion Brooks worked for eighteen years as a contributing columnist and news writer for *The New York Times*. In the late summer of 2008, Ms. Brooks threw out all of her shoes. "Most were elegant pumps with delicate heels," she wrote. "Some had rhinestones. A few were in glossy patent leather. But," she said, "they had to go" (Brooks 2008, R14).

In the process of giving up the shoes to Goodwill and replacing them with more comfortable "old lady shoes," Andrée Brooks learned how emotionally attached she'd become to her corporate footwear. Indeed, Brooks found herself going through the five classic stages of grief: (1) denial ("I'll wear high heels if it kills me!"), (2) anger ("How come Nancy can still wear platform shoes?"), (3) bargaining ("What if I don't wear the new ones *all* the time?"), (4) depression ("I look like Mickey Mouse"), and (5) acceptance ("I'm so comfortable, it's like walking on a cloud").

As we age, Ms. Brooks notes, our foot's natural padding thins, tendons and ligaments weaken, and arches fall flat. With age, pain while standing and walking leads us to buy more comfortable—

albeit less elegant—footwear. Since the shift from sexy to sensible is visible in the office, a transition to comfort can literally change who you are. Giving up narrow heels for wider flats sends a message for everyone to see: "My feet are grounded."

It took some grieving for Ms. Brooks to accept her down-to-earth status. But with comfortable shoes comes a different spin on the same message: "I have both feet on the ground." Having both feet on the ground may not be sexy, but the pragmatism, common sense, and realism suggested by sensible shoes are valued commodities for companies concerned with the bottom line.

The shoes send a corporate message of common sense. In her sensible footwear, Brooks worked as an associate fellow at Yale University and founded the Women's Campaign School to train women worldwide in the skills needed to win elective office. Ms. Brooks still visits fashionable shoe stores that sell chic, black patent-leather evening sandals, which she sometimes even buys. But she wears them only to small dinner parties where she needn't walk or stand—"Where I could once again dangle my feet with pride."

To Fill Someone Else's Shoes

So firm is the link between shoes and corporate identity that the idiom "fill (his or her) shoes," merits a definition in *The American Heritage Dictionary*: "To assume someone's position or duties" (Soukhanov 1992, 681). In 2006, just two years before he took over from Bill Gates as sole top executive at Microsoft, Steve Ballmer said, "Bill [Gates] and I are confident we've got a great team that can step up to fill his shoes and drive Microsoft innovation forward without missing a beat" (Clark 2006). Stepping up, filling shoes, and not missing a beat allude to energetic movements and the bipedal rhythm of walking, as in walking confidently toward a goal. Shortly before Mr. Ballmer became CEO, journalists commented figuratively on the "large size" of Bill Gates's shoes. One cautioned that "Steve Ballmer will have very big shoes to fill."

We know something, literally, about the shoes Steve Ballmer wears on his job, thanks to an interview he did with shoe mogul Dan Nordstrom. At the time of the interview, in 1999, Mr. Nordstrom was president and CEO of the world's largest shoe store, Nordstrom.com, with an inventory of some 20 million shoes. Explaining that he'd just purchased the shoes he was wearing from a Nordstrom department store, Steve asked Dan to show him around his virtual shop on the Internet.

Twenty million shoes are a lot to choose from, so Dan asked Steve a few questions about himself to help him pare down the choices from possible millions to just nine:

1. "Right now do you feel masculine, feminine, both, or none of the above?" (Answer: masculine)

2. "Would you most like to have tea with the Queen, star in an MTV video, run a four-minute mile, be king of the world, or work on your tan?" (Answer: be king of the world)

3. "Who would you rather have lunch with, Kenny from *South Park* or secret agent James Bond?" (Answer: Bond)

Now we know more about who you are, Dan explained. "You're a Wall Street guy, so we've narrowed you down [from 20 million] into a set of products which should be relevant to what you're looking for," Dan said in the interview. "So clearly," he continued, "here we've got the business shoes . . . and here's nine different items [to choose from]" (Ballmer 1999).

Photos of Steve Ballmer show him wearing dark brown, blunt-toed, thick-soled business oxfords much like the Banana Republic Positanos described above. Had he instead worn marshmallow-white basketball sneakers when he started his Microsoft career in 1980, odds are remote that he'd have eventually wound up as president and CEO. Indeed, Bill Gates might not have hired him to be the company's business manager in the first place. Each of the 20 million shoes Dan Nordstrom offered online had tales to tell. Certainly, marshmallow-white sneakers—if they were available— would have said the wrong thing.

Donna Sozio, the self-proclaimed "shoe-ologist" (she calls herself Dr. Sole) from Marina del Rey, California, is the founder of what she calls the "trickle-down theory" of men's shoes. As Ms. Sozio, author of *Never Trust a Man in Alligator Loafers* (2007), told LA.com's Melissa Heckscher, "A man's relationship to himself trickles down onto his relationship to his things. That trickles down to his relationship to everything else. The way he treats his shoes is an indication of how he's going to treat you" (Heckscher 2008).

Oversize basketball shoes, for example, reveal an insecure person who needs his group around him to survive. "Basketball is a group sport," Donna told Melissa. "He's probably more comfortable in groups. And big shoes are a sign of protection" (Heckscher 2008). His shoes say he would likely stay with his old friends rather than establish bonds with new partners or colleagues on the job.

"I used to think, 'Oh, Donna, don't be so superficial; they're just shoes,'" she explained. "But those same qualities I didn't like about the shoes showed up in my relationships three months, six months, nine months down the line. Relationships need maintenance, they need repair, they need to be shined up just like shoes do" (Heckscher 2008). Indeed, the shoes you wear in the workplace today say a lot about the shoes you may fill tomorrow.

Nowhere do shoes hold the key to identity more noticeably than in the workplace. Since they so precisely mirror your personality, shoes are among the most telling of all office signals. In the next chapter, we move from the body itself—from feet and toes, hands, eyes, shoulders, faces, lips, clothes, and hair—to the corporate places and spaces in which they're displayed continuously for eight hours a day, twelve months a year. How does your work space affect what your body does every day on the job?

Critical Dimensions
of Office Space

Every cubic inch of space is a miracle.
—Walt Whitman, "Miracles," in *Leaves of Grass*

If humankind's final frontier—space—is open, vast, and curved, office space is bounded, often cramped, and almost always linear. On the terrestrial plain, space is at such a premium that we slice and dice it into millions of mostly rectangular, boxlike rooms that colleagues perennially fight over. In the corporate world, a great deal of time is spent jockeying for premium parcels of office space.

Before I became a consultant, I spent many years working in offices. Since I'd been trained in anthropology and not in business, I viewed the office world through an exotic lens. Instead of bosses and managers, I saw tribal chieftains and headmen. Instead of bowling trophies and company rules, I saw totems and taboos. Weekly meetings were rituals, company picnics were corroborees (a type of Aboriginal ceremonial ritual). Corporate culture had a tangible look and feel, and gestures stood out to me as prominently as spoken and written words. As for office space itself, what I saw was not linear footage and square feet but corporate territory. I learned that the prime directive of office space is that we may not come and go everywhere as we please. There are cultural rules and biological boundaries—explicit as well as subtly implicit limits to observe—everywhere.

One of my office habitats (unnamed to protect the innocent) was a four-story brownstone in Washington, D.C., just north of Dupont Circle. My first-floor office had wraparound bay windows and a sweeping view of elm-tree-lined New Hampshire Avenue. I loved to look out at the elms and watch people stroll up and down the embassy-lined sidewalks.

Several months after I'd begun my director's job we hired a new director, Jayne, on my same job level. After glancing around my office, Jayne felt she needed it for her very own. Behind my back and behind closed doors, she lobbied our boss with reasons why it would be more efficient for *her* to be there, and for me to take the windowless office she'd been assigned. "David would be nearer his staff," she explained.

As an office rookie, I'd not yet learned how almost everything in business is negotiable. I didn't realize how easily, and efficiently, I could be negotiated out of my office space. On the other hand, our newcomer was a veteran who'd worked in the Washington bureaucracy for years and mastered its diplomatic ropes. Sensing, through basic animal instinct I imagine, that my space was in jeopardy, I ordered some office furniture to fill the small alcove to the left of my desk. I had the furniture installed immediately.

Since the new computer table was mine, and wouldn't fit anywhere but in the tiny alcove, my boss agreed I should stay put. Without the very visible material advantage—a mint-condition console with new-desk smell—I'm sure my colleague would have finagled my space. Since the boss was teetering, I'm grateful that my instincts kicked in with a solution. At the time, I realized that a tangible sign of possession was the perfect signal to send.

While Jayne and I later became good friends, she never failed to comment on my wonderful view of New Hampshire Avenue.

All I could do was smile, nod my head, and agree. To see out of my office space into the larger world was truly a gift.

Earliest Offices

Thousands of years before keyboards and cubicles, there was the first office. In this ancient workplace the dress code was even more relaxed than today's "office casual." The modal Mesopotamian office worker of circa 2,300 B.C. was an accountant called a *dubsar* or "tablet writer." He (most scribes were men) had long hair, a beard, a bared chest, and wore open-toed sandals beneath a skirtlike garment tied around his waist. He did not sit in a cubicle, and neither typed on a keyboard nor looked at a screen. His office had walls of mud bricks and mortar. He sat at a rectangular wooden desk near an open window. Sunlight, fresh air, and food aromas from a bustling walled city wafted through his workday. Unlike Mesopotamian farmworkers who toiled outside in heat and sun, scribes worked comfortably under roofs in shade.

A scribe named Likul occupied such an office. Likul (short for Likulubishtum) enjoyed his accounting job. He kept records of temple transactions, personnel, and supplies on hand. One of his duties was writing contracts, like the agreement he drew up for a client named Sini. Sini had bought a slave from Ilu for ten shekels of silver. Instead of recording the transaction on a laptop, Likul used a reed stylus, held in his right hand, to make wedge marks on palm-size tablets of damp clay held in his left. After hardening, the cuneiform-inscribed tablets were filed in ceramic jars as permanent records of the deal.

The daily routine of Likul's ancient office—meeting with clients, keeping records, writing reports, accounting for profits and losses— was little different from offices of today. We, too, assemble each workday in mostly rectangular rooms, sit at mostly rectangular desks, meet with clients, and record the results of our daily grind. Like Likul we use fine-motor, manipulative movements of our fingertips' tactile pads to seal deals permanently in writing. While the journey from stylus to mouse and keyboard seems immense, the brain modules enabling our fingers to work these office tools have remained the same. With training we, too, could learn cuneiform, just as Likul could learn Word.

We make educated guesses about Likul's ancient office based on findings of archaeologists. Archaeologists reveal the past by unearthing material remains—tangible and usually nonverbal "shreds and patches"—left behind after hundreds or thousands of years. In Likul's case, the remains were four-thousand-year-old pottery shards, brick-wall ruins, pictographic inlays, and inscribed clay tablets, one of which was Likul's cuneiform contract for the sale of the abovementioned slave.

Archaeologists complain about the sketchiness of their findings. Shreds and patches reveal but the barest outline of what went on so many years before. We do know that the Mesopotamian man, Likulubishtum, once worked in an office as a scribe. But exactly where was Likul's office? Who was his boss? How did Likul decorate, if at all, his office space? Did he get along with co-workers, play office politics, withhold information from clients? Was Likul a leader? Was he ultimately successful in his job? In archaeology such facts are frustratingly lost in time.

OFFICE SIGNALS

Signals beckon from every square inch of corporate space. A CEO's average-size four-hundred-square-foot office is five times bigger than the modal seventy-five-foot cubicle. If solid walls suggest permanence, moveable partitions imply "temporary." The dominant message of office space—bigger is better—is broadcasted every working day of the fiscal year. The message is relentlessly repeated, month after month, to drive home the point: Workers in big spaces are more important than workers in small ones.

Size doesn't matter to everyone, though. "I love my cubicle," Andrea, age twenty, writes in her personal blog. Not bothered by size differentials, she is happy in her cube. "I've had very few spaces in my life that are completely mine. Everything has a place in here and it stays there. And I keep it looking pretty and looking organized and I get plenty of comments—'Wow, your workspace is perfect'—and the like. You think I'm exaggerating, but I'm not. It's a good space" (Andrea 2006).

Andrea makes a telling point about office space. Whether you love or hate cubicles, how you decorate your seventy-five square feet sends an eye-catching message about who you are, how you feel, what you like, and where you'd rather be. Your space is a non-verbal newsletter about you.

Nondecorative signs within the cubicle can be telling as well. You may have noticed a small pink bottle of Pepto-Bismol on a co-worker's shelf. Though he doesn't talk about job pressure, the presence of a stomach remedy handily in reach could be a sign of chronic stress. Job stress is a reason why office-supply stores like McWhorter, in cubicle-filled Building J of Cisco Systems vast office complex in San Jose, California, stocks Pepto-Bismol. You needn't leave the building to replenish your supply, and colleagues again see the familiar sign of job discomfort on your shelf.

Controlled by the primitive enteric brain, job stress doesn't listen to reason. The enteric nervous system is a vast collection of nerve cells and circuits in the bowel area, of such complexity that it's been called the "second brain." In many ways independent of the brain proper, the enteric system has a mind of its own and expresses itself nonverbally in gut reactions on the job, such as sick feelings of nausea, urges to vomit, and abdominal pain. All three symptoms appear in cubicles on the average company's office floor, which some have facetiously called the Pepto-Bismol Playground. Invented in 1901 as a treatment for infant cholera, Pepto-Bismol is a sign of the times in today's pressure-filled workplaces.

Office Space for Forty-five Thousand

The size of your office building is a nonverbal statement about the importance of your job. One of the biggest office buildings in the world is the 102-story Empire State Building in New York City, deemed one of the Seven Wonders of the Modern World. Home to one thousand businesses, the Empire State Building welcomes approximately twenty-one thousand employees every workday.

Viewed from street level the nearly 1,454-foot-high building is so immense it dwarfs you, much as it dwarfed the mythical primate King Kong. You feel small and weak in its presence. Meanwhile, workers who ascend to their offices on a daily basis feel a sense of empowerment derived from the building's mass. The sheer size of it—2,158,000 square feet of office space—rubs off.

The Empire State Building's awe-inspiring verticality prompts what biologists call the *looming response*. The looming response is an automatic visual reaction that grants innate deference to objects of size. Massive human artifacts including skyscrapers, pyramids, and the Grand Coulee Dam appear magnified, powerful, and ominously threatening. That they loom so large gains immediate respect. Impressive natural features—high mountains, great boulders, and tall trees—are also viewed with wonder by native people who consider them sacred.

Sensing the nonverbal power of size, builders encode the looming effect into their designs. The 506-foot-high Deutsche Bank towers, 1,063-foot Eiffel Tower, and 1,451-foot Willis (formerly Sears) Tower were built large to inspire awe. To glorify himself, businessman Donald Trump opened the ninety-two-story Trump International

Hotel & Tower in Chicago, the tallest building constructed in the United States since the Sears Tower. In Bologna, Italy, powerful families of the twelfth century built towers merely to see whose was tallest. It's been estimated that dozens of functionally useless family towers dotted Bologna's cityscape. Just two remain today.

That the looming effect is alive and well in business is affirmed by Dubai property developer Nakheel's proposal to build a kilometer-tall skyscraper in Dubai with office space for forty-five thousand. The 3,274-foot office tower would eclipse the current world's tallest structure, the 2,717-foot Burj Khalifa, by more than 1,400 feet.

At my Washington, D.C., office building, our receptionist, Nicole, had a peculiar habit of attaching yellow sticky notes beneath her desk. Her desktop was neat, but chaos showed below it. Square yellow Post-it notes stuck everywhere, most with scribbles, some left blank. Nicole was likeable enough, but the confusion of so many stickies under her desk—on its stationary racks and inner panels—sent all the wrong signals.

"What's up with those sticky notes?" Everyone in the office commented, and behind her back some called Nicole a pack rat. Regardless of Nicole's actual performance, her décor made her *seem* less qualified than had she kept her desk clean. Everyone who noticed the unruly stash read it as an inappropriate or abnormal sign. Her compulsive Post-it notes made it hard for Nicole to be promoted to our office's next level, the position of program assistant. Her office signals had spoken, and she left us after barely three months.

It's one thing to post sticky notes on your own office furniture, and quite another to post them on a colleague's. When you place a yellow sticky on a co-worker's monitor, for example, you perhaps deliberately overstep your bounds. If the stickies around your own screen's perimeter are informational, bearing phone numbers and meeting dates, those stuck on the front of your screen overnight by others are blatantly territorial. You've been tagged by the office graffiti artist who attached an unspoken midnight message: BEFORE YOU DO ANYTHING ELSE READ ME!

Post-it note trespass is a recurrent event in many American offices. At his nonprofit organization's office in Northern Virginia, for example, Brad was greeted once a month by a pale yellow, three-inch-square note stuck on the middle of his computer screen. Yellow is a high-visibility hue used as a cautionary signal on roadways to attract notice. Though bright yellow suggests the sun's friendly glow, duller washed-out shades project an unpleasant and prickly mood of hostility. The message of Brad's monthly Post-it, written in black capital letters, was always the same: NEED YOUR MONTHLY REPORT!

The colleague who sent the message worked two doors down from Brad. Instead of stopping by to remind him in person, perhaps with a smile, he waited until Brad was out to stick the message on his screen. He needed to count coup by touching Brad's computer with his tacky note. This was the same man who placed memos on colleagues' chairs while they were at lunch. Face-to-face was not his style. As the Canadian communications theorist Marshall McLuhan famously noted, the medium is the message. For Brad, clearly, the Post-it note was a pain.

From interviews with office workers in educational, data-processing, and health-care fields, I've learned that many staffers feel an adrenal jolt when they first see sticky notes posted to their screens. The impertinent, sharp-edged little squares show someone has trespassed with a demand that can't wait. At the least, you must remove it to use your computer before you proceed.

If Post-it tag is an annoying ritual, it pales next to what some call Post-it warfare. In a serious sticky war, the messages are physically bold and visually strident. They call for swift counterattack. A manager unilaterally attacks with the seemingly benign message *Did you make your quota?* But he uses twenty Post-it notes—one oversize letter to a square—to spell out the question.

You come back from lunch and find your computer smothered in sticky notes. To retaliate you waste another twenty-five squares to answer, *Yes indeed I did make my quota!* Few office signals are as revealing of personal problems and corporate angst as these. Fortunately, such ritualistic battles are rare. Should you be victim to Post-it excess, defuse the matter with a face-to-face meeting. When you show up as the medium for your own message, you're more likely to manage a truce. Making eye contact is the first rule of diplomacy.

Just Say No to Knickknacks!

Obsessive posting of sticky notes is frowned upon by a new philosophy of workplace clutter control known as 5S. 5S advocates—the Ss stand for "sort," "straighten," "shine," "standardize," and "sustain"—strive to impress management, staff, and customers with the logical neatness and conspicuous cleanliness of the office. Paperwork should be filed, tools should be stored in specifically marked drawers, and knickknacks like bobblehead dolls and bouncy balls should be left at home. The idea is to create an efficient workspace with "reduced unreasonableness" that others can use in your absence.

5S came to America from the manufacturing sector in Japan. The Japanese word *seiri* (sorting) means getting rid of every nonessential item in your workspace, including personal artwork, family photos, and potted plants. *Seiton* (set in order) means arranging and storing items in the space for maximum efficiency. *Seisó* (sweeping) means keeping your work area relentlessly clean to reflect efficiency and enhance morale. *Seiketsu* (standardization) and *shitsuke* (discipline) make five.

Since U.S. office culture favors individualism over the Japanese focus on teamwork, there has been some confusion over 5S in the hundreds of offices that now subscribe to its ethic of neatness over personal expression. For example, at Kyocera Corporation's North American headquarters in San Diego, California—which started its own 5S program in April 2008—some employees needed direction from the company 5S inspector, Dan Brown (Jargon 2008, A1). Mr. Brown asked the accounting department to remove an unauthorized hook on a door, for instance, but okayed the presence of a whale figurine in a departmental cubicle.

"You have to figure out how to balance being too picky with upholding the purpose of the program," Brown said (Jargon 2008, A1). The unspoken message of a 5S office is that "we" matters more than "me." Few office signals are as culturally deep-seated as those favoring the group over the rugged individual. When knickknacks are out, teamwork is in.

Reading Triptych

A seemingly minor act in the office building—like installing a piece of sculpture—can have major meaning. Early in the 1960s, the placement at One Chase Manhattan Plaza in New York City of *Triptych,* a sculpture by Jason Seley, foretold of a dramatic power struggle to come at one of the world's largest financial institutions. The battle between Chase Manhattan Bank's CEO, David Rockefeller, who wanted change, and co-CEO George Champion, who wanted sameness, lasted a decade. Like handwriting on the wall, Seley's artistic alignment of chromium-plated bumpers came as a cautionary tale that the bank's top leaders were woefully conflicted.

A bumper is a metal or rubber bar placed at either end of an automobile to absorb the impact of collision. Detached from junkyard autos, Seley's bumpers were welded into a shiny piece of modern art. With the bumpers artfully standing together, humanlike, erect in upright posture, the sculpture was mounted on a red-tile wall on Chase headquarters concourse level.

Through business eyes, *Triptych* may be viewed as a yin-yang symbol of corporate cooperation (team alignment) and competition (ability to collide). Soon after Chase's board announced its joint appointment of the co-CEOs in October 1960, Seley's sculpture came to reflect the unspoken conundrum that Mr. Rockefeller and Mr. Champion simply could not see eye-to-eye—on anything. Since each had veto power over the other's decisions, nothing new got done.

Rockefeller wanted *Triptych* publicly displayed in the lobby as a nonverbal statement of Chase's modernity and forward thinking. But the sculpture's debut did not go as planned.

"The mistake we made," Rockefeller explained, "was putting it up during lunch hour." When alarmed Chase employees told Champion (who decorated his own office with historic, backward-looking antiques) that a futuristic "bunch of bumpers" was going up, he summarily vetoed the project. Without saying a word to Rockefeller, Champion had it removed and thus won the first battle of the artwork.

But he'd not won the war. David Rockefeller bided his time, purchased *Triptych,* and sent it out for a year on tour. Afterward, on a weekend when few were around headquarters, he had it reinstalled at Chase Manhattan Plaza, on the same concourse level where it remains to this day.

Rockefeller eventually took over as Chase's sole CEO. He was then able to make changes to internationalize the bank beyond Champion's conservative vision of keeping it national. As Rockefeller wrote in his *Memoirs:* "The 'bumpers' episode revealed a great deal about how George and I dealt with each other, most often by indirection and usually through intermediaries. As much as possible we avoided outright confrontation" (Rockefeller 2002, 177).

As an unwritten signal of Chase's discord at the highest level of power, Seley's sculpture had a prophetic, if silent, tale to tell.

Early in his tenure as co-CEO, David Rockefeller signaled his long-range intention to create a global bank. Those who read his signals knew what was likely to come next.

Conspicuous corporate artwork can be a silent signal of a company's changing fortune, outlooks, and worldview. What hangs on the walls can speak volumes about a firm's future prospects and health. The business may tell employees that all is well, but when management auctions off the corporate art collection, you can see the specter of problems ahead.

Consider what happened on October 17, 2005, for example, when New York commodities and futures brokerage Refco Inc. filed for Chapter 11 bankruptcy. In November and December of that year, Refco removed hundreds of pieces of coveted artwork from the walls of its New York and Chicago offices. In 2006, 321 of Refco's art photographs sold for $9.7 million at Christie's auction house. Though it was clear before the removal that Refco was in deep financial trouble, the act of their removal signaled that the company would never come back.

THINKING OUTSIDE THE RECTANGLE

Corporate space speaks in a clear, consistent, and continuous manner. To those who spend eight-hour days together in the company's average-size, 250-square-foot common areas, space may feel too close for comfort. For prehistoric context, consider our hunter-gatherer ancestors who spent workdays on an estimated 440-square-mile expanse of African savannah. Compared to open savannahs, today's workplace can feel terribly cramped.

The modal modern office is what I call a rectangular status space, or RSS. RSS design consists of a grid-patterned scheme of separate walled-off, rectangular offices, the sizes of which reflect a worker's status in the firm. Bigger, as a rule, means better.

A company I worked with fit RSS to a T. When they moved from an inner-city town house to a high-rise office building in the suburbs, their status spacing didn't change. The boss's corner office was still biggest, with windows on two walls. Lower-echelon executives had offices half as big, with windows on one wall. Per the RSS metric, those executives were meant to feel half the size of their boss. Support personnel sat in the interior of the firm's office space, in rectangular cubicles roughly a third the size of executive offices, with partitions, no walls, and no windows. The receptionist sat in the loneliest cubicle of all, spatially removed from everyone, in the lobby by the glass front doors. At the very center of the office suite was a large conference room— roomy, rectangular, and windowless—which sat vacant most of the time.

Picking up on the signals, vendors and visitors to the new office sensed something wrong. They saw demoralized shoulders, uninspired eyes, and blank faces. They heard weary, monotone voices, or silence. They correctly sensed an ambient mood of depression. Workers spent most workdays alone in rectangles, and walked slowly through hallways as if walking underwater. There was a palpable lack of energy, little collaboration, and no team spirit.

To buoy the company office, board members recommended a team-building exercise. Staff met with trainers in the conference room, and learned ways to be more collaborative. From the very first session workers felt better. Enthusiasm sounded in voices, and excitement showed in smiles. Yet each time workers left the training and returned to their beige walls, gray carpets, and rectangular spaces filled with unerringly angular in-boxes, file cabinets, and desks, the feeling of togetherness went away. They were again at the mercy of their right-angled, squared-off, relentlessly partitioned space. The built-in hierarchy and room dividers kept them structurally apart.

This ailing company needed a nonverbal makeover. The structural design caused functional distress. The office should have recycled—gotten rid of—the walls and partitions and opened up the conference room for added space. They should have let the sunshine in for more workers to see; repainted beige walls with energetic yellows and oranges; torn out the industrial-thin carpeting; polished the concrete floor; and exposed the ceilings, loft style. They should have added softer furniture, rounder tables, shared-task areas, and informal visiting stations. Moreover, they should have had fewer assigned offices and cubes, and let employees use private-thinking spaces as needed. Their people should have been able to move freely through an open office, and interface with colleagues to learn what they did on the job.

But there was no redesign. The office stayed in rectangular mode for years after my work there was done. Traditional RSS design had prevailed. Eventually, many staff resigned or retired, and the publications program, the firm's biggest department, was outsourced. Might a change in office space have boosted collaboration and team spirit? Based on what many companies are currently doing, the likely answer is yes. Increasingly, companies are successfully redesigning and empowering staff to think outside the rectangle.

An example is Cisco Systems, the multinational networking and communications technology firm in San Jose, California. Cisco managed to revamp its rectangular floor plan and create a collaboration-friendly space in Building 14 at its San Jose headquarters campus. Soon after, the prototype workspace was installed elsewhere in the United States and in Osaka, Japan.

Introduced to Building 14 in February 2006, Cisco's "connected office" had corrected for all the design-feature problems at the firm outlined above. Taking out walls and getting rid of formal conference rooms, private offices, and cubicles enabled Cisco employees to literally think outside the box. With no assigned seating, work spaces, or desks, and with shared phones and wireless PCs, employees could be more collaborative on the job. Staffers could work on teams of two or more, or work alone, depending on the project at hand. The percentage of workers who were "extremely satisfied" with the new design rose to 35 percent, nearly double the 18 percent measured for the company's previous office design. As Cisco's vice president of connected real estate, Mark Golan, noted, "Almost everyone who comes through Building 14 smiles and nods their heads" (Bacon 2007).

BEST OFFICE SPACES

What are the signs of a healthy office? What should you look for to gauge if you'd be happy working at the company you applied to? Consider some positive signals identified by Winning Workplaces of Evanston, Illinois, a nonprofit whose mission is "to help organizations create great workplaces." In the best workplaces you will see signs that the company is about more than just work. Here are some things to look for:

- *A Ping-Pong Table and Soccer Balls* The presence of a Ping-Pong table or soccer ball in an office is a positive sign that co-workers not only work together but get along well enough to play together. Both signs are visible at Decagon Devices, Inc., a manufacturer of scientific instruments in Pullman, Washington. Like each of the offices profiled, Decagon was selected as one of the fifteen "Top Small Workplaces" by Winning Workplaces and *The Wall Street Journal*. To build teamwork on breaks, Decagon office mates challenge each other to Ping-Pong games and soccer matches. Unlike many companies, Decagon encourages employees to socialize at work.

- *Homemade Meals* Do you see employees sharing home-cooked food? In a work environment, food sharing is a positive sign. When the edibles have been prepared at home, sharing is even more positive. The underlying message is that staff members care for each other as family. At Decagon, for instance, workers have regular Wednesday lunches with food dishes brought from home. Co-workers eat together as a group, socialize, and share information about the company. For primates, mealtimes are the most sociable times of day. Anxiety from the ambient fight-or-flight mode is replaced by calmer rest-and-digest feelings that foster camaraderie and teamwork.

- *Sit-down Coaching Sessions* When you see staff sitting down with managers face-to-face on a weekly basis, it's a sign of quality management. In some companies, sitting down one-on-one with a boss happens only once a year at the performance appraisal. Such is not the case, happily, at Integrated Project Management Company (IPM) in Burr Ridge, Illinois, where workers sit down with bosses once a week to discuss progress and work performance. IPM's CEO, Richard Panico, likens the regular sit-down meetings to personal coaching. Because honesty and integrity are stressed at weekly meetings, IPM employees don't lose sight of ethical concerns on the job. Had bosses at Enron, Arthur Andersen, and Lehman Brothers sat down one-on-one more often with employees, these companies might not have failed.

- *Giving Back* Do you see people volunteering for charitable causes apart from work? Does the company set aside office space for employees to work on projects for organizations like Unicef, March of Dimes, and Red Cross? This is a positive sign that it shows allegiance to causes other than the bottom line. At Redwoods Group Inc., a specialty insurer based in Morrisville, North Carolina, employees do at least forty hours of volunteer work per year—on company time. Additionally, Redwoods asks workers to get involved in community cleanups and food drives. Company founder Kevin Trapani said that Redwood needed to give its employees "something to feel really good about when they come to work" (Spors 2008, R9).

BE SAFE IN OFFICE SPACE

Late on a Thursday afternoon I was sitting in my Washington, D.C., office at my computer. A colleague came in and took the chair next to my desk. "They're going to let him go," she said in a low voice. "Tonight."

"Who?"

"Bart in accounting," she answered.

"Bart? Our junior accountant? Why?"

Bart was someone I liked. He always looked up from his desk to greet me with a smile when I walked by. He always wore a pressed white shirt and a colorful tie. He always had something nice to say, with a sense of humor, in a clear, soft voice. He never said anything bad about anybody in the office. He kept his desk clean.

"Why Bart?" I asked again.

"I don't know why," my colleague answered, "but I know it's tonight, and I don't want to be here when it happens. Okay, see you tomorrow."

Tomorrow came with a surprise. On Friday morning I walked my usual route up New Hampshire to the office. As I crossed the street near my building, going with the green light, I saw two policemen loitering on the front stoop. What grabbed my attention more than the sight of the police, however, were the dripping globs and blotches of bright yellow paint splashed on the brownstone's walls, windows, and wooden front door. Two gallons, at least, of viscous, semigloss latex had been splattered on our building. Since my own office window took some paint as well, the vandalism seemed personal.

"Bart!" I thought. Then I wondered why his name so easily popped into my mind. I'd always liked him and he'd never done me harm. But it was Bart, indeed, the police said. Very early, in Friday-morning darkness, Bart and his uncle had defiled our building with random splatters of loud paint. The uncle had already confessed. Bart, meanwhile, had fled to Philadelphia back to his boyhood home, and a minor episode of workplace violence ended quietly, without anyone getting seriously hurt. We never saw our junior accountant again.

That morning the question in my and every co-worker's mind was, Would Bart come back with a shotgun? Though rare in the workplace, violent incidents of revenge can and do happen. Consider the case of another fired and disgruntled accountant, Anthony LaCalamita, who did come back to his office with a gun.

Like Brad, Anthony LaCalamita III, thirty-eight, seemed even-tempered at work. His boss Paul Riva, one of three victims LaCalamita shot in the accounting office, testified at trial that Mr. LaCalamita "worked diligently" and was "always polite" (Anonymous 2008a). The days of Anthony's politeness, however, were numbered.

On April 9, 2007, former employee Anthony LaCalamita entered the second-floor offices of Gordon Advisors Accounting Firm in Troy, Michigan, armed with a shotgun. Anthony had just been laid off from his accounting job at Gordon Advisors the week before. Once inside the building he walked—"boldly," prosecutors said—past the reception desk and went without hesitation into Alan Steinberg's office (Anonymous 2008a). Mr. Steinberg, forty-eight, instinctively stood up to show a larger profile and defend his office space. Thinking the shotgun unreal, Steinberg tried to push it away. Anthony quickly shot his ex-boss in the hip and seriously wounded him.

LaCalamita walked farther down the hall, past crouching ex-colleagues with whom he made eye contact, to the doorway of his second ex-boss, Paul Riva, forty-seven. Perhaps because she got in the way, he shot and killed the company receptionist, Madeline Kafoury, sixty-three, in Riva's doorway. He then stepped inside Riva's office, fired a wounding blast into his chest—"immediately," Riva testified—and then, police reported, "calmly left the building."

In Anthony LaCalamita's case, as in junior accountant Bart's, no preincident indicators were seen in the workplace. There were no visible signs, in either office, that either accountant would or could do harm. At work, both Anthony and Bart seemed polite and perfectly even-tempered.

How can workplace incidents like these happen without warning signs? It's because the workplace is a stage that is preset for deception. From résumé to job application to interview, from office demeanor to office dress—at every step in getting and keeping a job—deception is built into the process. Résumés highlight strengths and hide weaknesses. Interviews expound good qualities while concealing the bad. On the job, sleeves cover the tattoo you reveal after hours. Workplace dramaturgy is choreographed to make you seem fit for the job—and to conceal some of the ways in which you're not.

Such preincident indicators as grabbing, slapping, or punching are more visible outside work than in the office. In the months leading up to his shootings, Anthony LaCalamita used a crowbar to attack a thirty-year-old man, hitting him in the head and jabbing him with the heavy steel tool. Had his bosses at the accounting firm known of these aggressive acts, they might have anticipated Anthony's invasion of their office space. For the typical two-week danger period—the interval in which most revenge attacks take place after a triggering event, such as getting fired—they could have kept their doors locked and hired a security guard as a temp.

Your office space is not likely to erupt in violence, nor should your employer be expected to behave as a law-enforcement officer to protect you on the job. Nonetheless, the workplace can be a highly stressful, volatile, and overcrowded habitat where emotions can run dangerously high.•When colleagues are fired or laid off, be extra alert for preincident signs warning of possible attack. As Mark Ames explores in his book *Going Postal* (2005), workplace shootings are becoming ever more common.

———

The look and feel of office space, and what goes on within its three dimensions, have profound effects on workers. In many respects, the modern office habitat is unnatural for a species that's spent more than 99 percent of its prehistory wandering, hunting, and gathering in wide-open spaces. In this chapter, we've charted some of the hidden dimensions of office space that contribute to health, happiness, and safety on the job. In the next chapter we'll take a fine-grained look at a single business meeting to decode its nonverbal agenda. In the workplace, gestures are truly as important as words.

TEN

A Meeting Decoded

Thus far in *Your Body at Work* you have learned to sight-read faces, eyes, hands, shoulders, hairstyles, clothing, and even shoes. Sight-reading, the perceptive observation of nonverbal cues, enables you to see beneath words in order to fathom unspoken meanings, agendas, and moods. A colleague's pursed lips reveal hidden disagreement. Intermittent eye movements to the right or left show a colleague is processing your words. A suddenly lifted shoulder speaks of doubt. Indeed, in every office there is meaning to be found in every body.

Let's look now at how bodies behave in the formal context of a business meeting. A meeting is typically held at a conference table. Attendees usually adopt the preferred resting posture of primates, sitting down, and may remain comfortably seated for hours at a time. Since torso stature is more uniform than standing height (the latter varies more with leg length), there is no height advantage around the table. When seated, human beings appear to be more or less all the same size. Beneath the tabletop, bodies below the waist are hidden and visual attention shifts upward to faces, shoulders, and hands. These three bodily areas—along with the star attraction, the verbal voice box or larynx—play leading roles. To learn how they work together as an ensemble, consider the "The Natural History of a Meeting," a play conducted in three short acts:

THE NATURAL HISTORY OF A MEETING

Prelude

3:50 P.M.

The conference room sits dark and empty. It is spacious, with beige walls, no distracting artwork, and a thin gray carpet. Resting heavily on the carpet is the dominant prop in the room, an imposing, solid conference table with chromium legs and a thick tabletop of brown wood. Upon its well-worn surface, the stage is set for a weekly staff meeting scheduled to begin promptly at 4:00 P.M. You are cordially invited to sit in on the meeting to follow its drama and sight-read its nonverbal cues.*

Act I: An Offhand Commandment

3:55 P.M.

A stooped, white-haired gentleman in a light gray suit enters the conference room. Al is the company's CEO. In his midfifties, he has a noticeably labored gait. He bends forward stiffly at the waist from chronic back pain. His face shows the classic signs of pain: narrowed eye openings, slightly raised cheeks (as his orbital muscles contract in a wince), pulled-down eyebrows, barely noticeable wrinkles at the bridge of his nose, and a mildly raised upper lip. Since Al's pain level is higher than normal this afternoon, he appears to be in a foul mood. He flips on the overhead neon lights and stoop-walks another thirty feet, the length of the board table,

*This chapter includes my observations of several meetings of one company's central management team. For instructional purposes, these observations are amalgamated into the single meeting described here. Names have been changed to protect the participants' privacy, and the company name shall remain anonymous.

to his place at its head. Uncharacteristically early, Al takes his seat.

3:59 P.M.

Members of the management team begin to arrive. CFO Franz, Al's right-hand man, along with comptroller, Margaret, walk through the door. Next to arrive are the "like-minded three" (so called because they almost always agree with one another, and not with the boss), Sheri, Bev, and Raymond. The last to arrive—soft-spoken Julia, laconic Lucy, and mercurial Charles—join colleagues at the table. All ten actors, including Al's secretary, Sharon, are now seated at the conference table. An uncomfortable meeting is about to begin.

4:00 P.M.

The conference room is unusually quiet on this November day. There's none of the smiling, chatting, joking, or convivial laughter of meetings past. The somber mood is in response to Al's tightly compressed lips, formal suit jacket (which he usually leaves in his office), and narrowed, unwelcoming eyes. He avoids the group's eyes, and his own stay glued to his folded hands, which are resting on papers spread in a semicircle before him. Taking their cue from Al's sullen look, team members dart anxious glances at each other and remain silent, as if waiting for the proverbial "other shoe" to drop.

4:01 P.M.

"Please close the door," Al says in an icy tone. From where he was sitting, on Al's immediate right, Franz walks the length of the table to close the door. Ordinarily left open, the door shuts with a thud. In the conference room's silence, the thud sounds an ominous warning of bad news to come. As if looking for the fabled other shoe, all eyes but Al's gaze up and around, and look uneasily at each other. The meeting has scarcely begun yet is already filled with fear and loathing.

4:02 P.M.

After another sixty-second pause, Al brings the meeting to order. His calculated hesitation makes what he says more dramatic. As anthropologist Edward T. Hall notes in his book *The Silent Language,* "Time speaks." As a nonverbal message, according to Hall, waiting time in the United States has eight levels of duration: immediate, very short, short, neutral, long, very long, terribly long, and forever (Hall 1959). For those in the meeting room today, the boss's short pause takes forever.

Abruptly, Al's larynx begins buzzing and his mouth fills with words. He nods his head forward to give emphasis to the words. A head nod is a vertical, up-and-down movement of the skull used to emphasize an idea, an assertion, or a key speaking point. Emphatic nods while speaking indicate powerful feelings of conviction and certainty. The human head nod originates from the reptilian *head-bobbing* display, used aggressively by lizards to proclaim their physical presence in a group—as if to say, "Notice me, I am here!"

As Al nods his head, his right hand unclasps and releases the left, rises above the scattered papers on the table, and flips over so the palm lies parallel to the tabletop. The hand's palm-down position reveals an adamant state of mind, as if to say, "I am serious!" Al's hand now moves forward, as if reaching for the opposite end of the table. It seems to hang there, stiffly outstretched for all to see. Five fingers fully extend, and his palm hovers four inches above the table's surface. As he dramatically holds the gesture outward, Al says, "Starting *today*, I will no longer accept late reports."

All eyes focus on Al's palm-down hand splay as it takes center stage. Without actually touching the tabletop, he moves the gesture up and down, like a judge's gavel, to drive the point home: "Starting *today* . . ."

Judging from his gesture—there are definitely *no* shoulder shrugs here—and lower tone of voice, Al clearly means what he says. Three seats down the table, on Al's right, Sheri lifts her shoulders. The movement is slight but perceptible. Her shrug suggests a diffident or submissive stance vis-à-vis Al. In the context of his vocal pronouncement, Sheri's shoulders defer to Al's authoritative hand. Meanwhile, Charles, who sits next to Sheri on his left, leans back in response to Al's edict. He reacts by folding both arms high upon his chest. Charles's sudden backward lean and crossed arms suggest feelings of defensiveness and dissention. Before the boss reached out his palm-down gauntlet, Charles had been leaning forward with both arms on the table. "Starting *today* . . ." clearly registers in Charles's brain, and his body shares the news.

Sheri and Charles respond to Al's words with defensive body movements. Both are guilty of late reports, while their co-workers are consistently on time. Bodies of the latter staff members stay as they were before Al's decree, leaning forward with elbows, forearms, and hands on the table. Innocent of late charges, their bodies relax. Elbows spread out, hands let go of each other, curled wrists extend and straighten. It sinks in among the guilt-free that in this meeting, at least, they're no longer at risk. Lips loosen, knitted brows unwrinkle, and the world is good again.

Lucy, who sits next to Al's secretary, Sharon, asks a question. As Lucy speaks, her right hand flips upward to reveal a fully opened palm. She reaches it forward and out to Al, as if offering him a coin to pluck from the palm of her hand. Like Sheri's lifted shoulders, Lucy's palm show makes a submissive appeal. Palm-up gestures like hers are commonly used in response when employers give palm-down signs. A palm-up hand appeals for amends to be made, as in, "Let's come together again."

A buzzing sound issues from Lucy's larynx, filling her mouth with words: "Can we turn in late reports," she asks with a rolled-up palm, "if we've been out of the office on the road?"

"Good question," Al answers. "I guess that's the one exception." He matches Lucy's palm-up with one of his own and adds a shrug of his shoulders. Seeing the two nonaggressive body movements, staffers sense a thaw. Al's demeanor now hints of deference and he seems to calm down. Seeing Al's open palm and lifted shoulders as signs of détente, Sheri and Charles rejoin colleagues by leaning their forearms, wrists, and hands back on the conference table. Congruence in sitting postures reflects congruence in the group's state of mind. Like-minded colleagues think, feel, and sit like each other. The staff meeting has shifted from fear and loathing to solidarity and goodwill. Even Al shows a smile.

Sharon's minutes summarize the meeting's first quarter hour in one sentence: *Al directed that late reports will no longer be accepted, unless managers are out of town or on assignment.* In contrast to the succinct minutes, you have watched bodies perform a longer, more dramatic one-act show. In fifteen minutes the meeting moved, like a morality play, from fear to salvation and then a semblance of normalcy. If all you had were Sharon's notes, you'd be at a loss to explain what happens next, in Act II, when a controversial agenda item threatens to wreck company morale. Using Act I's body language as a baseline, you will clearly see the strong emotions that threaten to fragment the team.

Act II: A Heated Debate

4:17 P.M.

Al stands, removes his gray suit jacket, and hangs it on the back of his chair. The formality of his appearance dissipates. He sits down again and introduces the next item on the meeting agenda.

"Franz," Al says, "would you please start us on this?" "This" is the second go-round on a most unpopular issue, that of "at-will" employment.

4:18 P.M.

Franz opens a black vinyl notebook, adjusts his glasses, and glances down at a type-filled page. He rubs his nose with a knuckle. Now Franz's larynx begins to buzz as words fill his mouth. He leans fully forward, out over the notebook, as if to get closer to colleagues across the way. His body lean is overdone and borderline aggressive. Al now leans forward as well, imitating Franz's overzealous body posture. Acting alike shows the two men are together and on the same page.

"As you know," Franz says, "our board has asked that we explore the at-will model for our company." He speaks slowly at first, softly and deliberately. His face is parked in neutral above the notebook, without expression, his lips in repose, and his eyes saccade (or rapidly shift) from listener to listener across the table. Fingertips resting calmly on his notebook's open page, Franz's hands are motionless. "The board feels," he goes on, "that an at-will model could better serve our company. They asked us to look into it."

4:19 P.M.

The mood in the room shifts from one of solidarity and goodwill to guarded opposition. Charles leans back. He scoots his chair out from under the table and crosses his legs, right ankle over left knee. Perhaps to show a bigger profile, he reveals more of his body to make a point, as in, "You don't scare me." He retakes the defensive, crossed-arms stance he adopted earlier in Act I, and shoots a fixed gaze at Franz's face. Now Sheri leans back and crosses her arms. Her lips tighten and her lip corners begin to droop as she gazes up the table at Franz. And now, following suit, Bev leans back. Her upper body angles away from both Franz and Al as she twists away to her left. Bev's eyes, though, remain locked onto Franz's.

Margaret leans back. Julia and Lucy lean back. Everyone in the room leans back now, except Franz and Al, who lean too far forward as Franz makes his case. Sharon leans forward, too, but only to take notes. Her forward lean is about function, not attitude. Nonverbally, the weekly meeting coalesces into opposing camps, those for at-will and those against, with Sharon abstaining. The vote shows clearly in the direction of body lean, and the nays seem to have it.

4:20 P.M.

"As you know," Franz continues, "our company may need to downsize or restructure at some point in time, and the at-will option gives us flexibility to do this." As he makes his case for adding an at-will clause to the company handbook, his right hand leaves the black notebook and launches a preemptive salvo of palm-down strikes. In unison, all five fingertips adamantly tap on the conference table. Franz senses resistance in his colleagues' leaning away, tense lips, and hostile eyes, and his mood turns prickly. His hand balls into a fist, and he stabs the tabletop with a stiffly extended index finger on its surface to make a point.

4:24 P.M.

Known for his angry outbursts, Charles reaches out a palm-down gesture of his own. "Our handbook says we can only be terminated 'for cause.' It can't just be arbitrary," he argues. After the words leave his mouth, Charles's hand folds back into the arm-cross from whence it came.

Sheri's petite right hand reaches out its own flipped-down palm. There is no shoulder shrug this time as she says, with anger in her voice, "I don't know about this. We've *always* had due process in our jobs. That's a *big section* in our handbook." She ratchets her palm-down hand up and down to the assertive beat of her words.

Margaret's big hand now flips open and over, palm down, and reaches out as if to swat Franz's words as she would swat a mosquito. "At-will means we can all be fired for no reason at all. That gives a boss just too much power," Margaret says, emotionally shaking her head from side to side. The head shake is a universal sign of negation and refusal. In Margaret's case, it means she truly feels at-will employment is wrong. One of the neck muscles that shakes the head—the *sternocleidomastoid*—is an emotional muscle that responds to gut feelings and moods. In tandem with her words, Margaret's head shake rings true. She has gut issues with this possibility.

Now Al's palm-down hand joins the fray. It reaches out with the weight of final authority. "We'll need to rewrite the handbook," he says. "You'll be asked to sign a statement acknowledging your at-will status." Al's voice sounds low and angry as he begins to lose his temper. He senses his side has already lost the public-relations war. Judging from words and body language, he and Franz have not won the hearts and minds of staff.

Lucy gives an exasperated laugh and says, "You can't make us sign it! No way." Her right hand flips palm down to slap the tabletop. "Why would anybody sign it? That's just crazy." Human laughter is a rhythmic vocalization that greatly varies in form, duration, and loudness. In attack mode, laughter may be directed at enemies and persons one disagrees with or dislikes, as a form of *aggression-out*. Mocking, aggressive laughter resembles the *group-mobbing* vocalizations of higher primates. Lucy's outburst of annoyed laughing reveals how heated the discussion has become. Colleagues haven't hit each other yet, but they've slapped the tabletop as if intending to.

The at-will discussion goes on for twenty minutes. Dueling hands fill the air space above the table. Some land on the table's surface with audible thumps. Clear nonverbal lines have been drawn. Those for making the change lean forward, those opposed lean back. With all of their bodies frozen into such frankly antagonistic poses, the meeting fragments—two against seven—along managerial lines.

Al finally has had enough. The pain in his face is now more from the meeting than from his aching back. "Okay, we'll take this up again next week," he concludes.

And, just as suddenly as the tension surrounding at-will employment arose, it is suddenly defused. Al raises his hand to quiet the meeting. A popping sound comes from the serving table in back, behind his chair. Franz had gotten up from the table as the discussion was winding down, and he has just uncorked two bottles of wine.

Act III: A Glad Announcement

4:38 P.M.

"We can deal with all this stuff next time. I know it's a problem," Al says to placate. "Now, though, I have a birthday to announce! Happy birthday, Charles! Would you like red or white?"

4:39 P.M.

In a matter of moments, with Al's brief announcement the meeting's mood changes from "if looks could kill" glares to happy birthday cheer. Business meetings can change direction at the drop of a hat, but this one is likely to cause a case of corporate whiplash. Suddenly, corn chips, chocolate cake, and ice cream come out. White paper plates, white plastic spoons and forks, and red, white, and blue napkins emerge. Coffee, fruit juice, and semivintage cabernet and chardonnay beckon.

When you wield the same white plastic forks, eat the same foods off the same paper plates, drink the same beverages from identical cups, and use the same colored napkins as others to wipe your hands and mouth, you feel subliminally bonded to a team. The biological basis underlying this corporate feeling of togetherness is *isopraxism,* the reptilian principle of uniting by doing the "same thing."

Examples of isopraxism (the word means "same behavior" in Greek) include the simultaneous head nodding of lizards, the group gobbling of turkeys, and the synchronous preening of birds. Certainly head nodding and hair preening, and some might even say group gobbling, go on routinely in staff meetings. Isopraxism among human beings, Anne H. Soukhanov writes in her book *Word Watch,* "is manifested in the hand-clapping of a theater audience and, on a larger scale, in historical mass migrations, in mass rallies, violence, and hysteria, and in the sudden widespread adoption of fashions and fads" (Soukhanov 1993, 135). Around the world in business, eating and drinking together is the universal formula to bring people together.

Eating and drinking elicit the *relaxation response,* a pleasant feeling of calmness and well-being experienced as the heart rate slows, smooth muscles contract, and glands secrete while the body digests. Physiologically, relaxation through food consumption—the rest-and-digest response—is a rudimentary model for the sensation of human happiness.

Many involuntary nonverbal signs—such as constricted pupils, glistening eyes (brought on by moisture from the tear glands), slowed breathing, warm and dry palms, forward leaning, and supinated palms—are visible in visceral feelings of the rest-and-digest response.

4:41 P.M.

Rest-and-digest is plainly visible here in the conference room. Lips curve upward in smiles. Voices lighten as eyes make relaxed and more civil contact. Staffers lean forward over white paper plates. Open hands wave happy birthday to Charles. The office party ends at 5:00 P.M., but the wine drinkers often stay in the boardroom until 6:00 on special occasions such as these. In moderation, spirits infuse the body's relaxation response with even greater good cheer.

4:45 P.M.

Nobody gives palm-down gestures above the board table now. Hands turn upward to show open palms instead. Shoulders shrug with light comments, polite laughter, and small talk. Colleagues open their minds and bodies, and face each other instead of cringing, turning away, or leaning back. The fight-or-flight response wanes with cake and ice cream as bodies shrug off the weight of another staff meeting.

5:01 P.M.

The conference room is once again empty. None chose to stay after 5:00 today. The air is filled with lingering aromas of chocolate, coffee, and cabernet. So have a final glass of wine if you'd like and then head for the train. And be thankful you don't work here. The pace is frenetic.

Though nowhere recorded in the official minutes, body language disclosed that in one hour's time a small group of human primates moved from a state of anxiety and loathing, to near corporate meltdown, to rest-and-digest. The bodies spoke clearly, revealing what words did not—unvoiced feelings and alliances along with unspoken attitudes and moods. Those who watched body language would no doubt agree: The company dramatized in this three-act play has challenges ahead. "A house divided against itself," Abraham Lincoln (1809–1865) wrote, "cannot stand." As we've seen throughout *Your Body at Work,* bodies cannot lie.

In the context of a business meeting, there's a world of difference in a lifted or level shoulder, an upturned or downturned palm, a torso's forward or backward lean. As you witnessed, these body parts are central players in "The Natural History of a Meeting." By objectively observing them in your own workplace, as you would in a play, you'll be able to decode the dramaturgy of even the most tangled corporate plot. In the next chapter, you will learn to decipher the body language of your employer, the boss. Using animal psychology and the nonverbal techniques of lion tamers, even the most difficult boss can be turned into the perfect lady or gentleman.

ELEVEN

No Bad Bosses

I find that if you stay with your hand relaxed, the dog spits it out rather than bites it, but I know this is not easy for everyone to do.
—Barbara Woodhouse, *No Bad Dogs*

What do dogs and bosses have in common? Both are mammals, both have set routines, and both can be trained. Richard Kelly, owner of K-9 Heroes in Silver Spring, Maryland, says the central problem in dog training is lack of borders. If you give a dog a clear and firm set of rules—if you tell a dog he's not allowed to step over the line for any reason, ever—and if you are consistent and reward good behavior, your dog will calm down and like you better. He knows that as long as he stays inside these borders, life will be fine (Laskas 1988).

LYNN'S PROBLEM BOSS

"My boss follows me around the building if I am out of my chair for more than ten minutes," Lynn complained. "The funny thing is, he thinks I don't notice! I could go to the community mailboxes, then to the restroom, and if ten minutes have elapsed, there he is, like clockwork, outside the bathroom at the water fountain. This happens in one form or another DAILY, if not more often" (Anonymous 2007b). Lynn's is a fairly typical complaint. Her boss is a micromanager whose compulsion is to oversee an employee's every movement. To overcome his compulsive behavior, Lynn's boss needs to be trained.

Training a boss, like training a dog or taming a lion, requires consistency and a steady gaze. Bosses are primates who respond to direct eye contact as a sign of strength. As mammals, bosses need clear and consistent treatment or they'll become neurotic and confused. Boss training is neither combative nor a test of wills. Using nonverbal cues and animal psychology—the same principles employed by dog, lion, and tiger trainers—even the most neurotic boss can be contained. You can turn a lion's den into a circus cage where the boss may be trained to follow your lead.

Assuming Lynn is not a problem employee, I'd advise her to show her boss, John, that his penchant for following her is out of bounds. Beginning today, whenever she leaves the restroom and catches John at the water fountain, Lynn should look him in the eye, reach an authoritative, palm-down hand toward him, and say, "Hi, John." Recall from chapter 4 that palm-down gestures are powerfully assertive. Like TV pundits, dog trainers use palm-down cues to accent words. For the latter, words include, "No!" "Sit!" "Down, boy!"

John is not a canine, and he may not consciously register Lynn's message any more than a dog would. Yet he will register Lynn's eye contact and commanding palm with the same modules of mammalian brain as employed by canids. Dogs and human beings read direct stares and commanding palms as signs to be reckoned with. To reach a cumulative effect, these assertive cues should be given repeatedly and consistently at the point of offense. For Lynn, this would be outside the bathroom at the water fountain, should John be lurking there as she leaves. Her firm hand will show the boss he's not to step over the line. Each time he follows her at work, he will see Lynn's hand: "No!" Instead of hearing it in words, he will see a gesture even a dog understands: "Down, boy!"

Superstar circus tamer, Gunther Gebel-Williams, knew that as dangerous as training a wild animal can be, it's preferable to dealing with an unpredictable creature liable to pounce without warning. To survive in a lion cage, Gebel-Williams learned that consistency is key: "You cannot be a dreamer with animals. You cannot take a day off. You must be the same person every day" (Capuzzo 1991, C8).

Captive animals regard cages as their personal territory. Entering either a tiger's cage or a boss's office carries some risk of, respectively, attack or verbal abuse. Entering either space violates a zoological zone known as *critical distance*. An animal's need for this critical distance is why people who climb into zoo enclosures are mauled, even by "friendly" lions, tigers, and bears.

The boss tamer's art is one of strategic prodding, parrying, advancing, and retreating. When handling your boss, as when handling a lion, the greatest danger is complacency. Keeping the more powerful animal off balance atop a pedestal takes daily alertness and vigilance to nonverbal signals, month after month.

A Very Bad Boss

Few have had a boss who behaved as badly as Greg DePalma. Mr. DePalma, the septuagenarian chief of Mafia operations in New York's Westchester County, allegedly used a power tool on the head of a colleague he thought had stolen from him.

"Greg DePalma, I would best describe him as the devil incarnate. A very evil man," says retired FBI agent Jack Garcia. Mr. Garcia, who operated undercover as "Jack Falcone," a fictitious Italian American mobster, "worked" for Mr. DePalma and gained such trust that he was invited to become an official member of the Mafia organization. Garcia recounts his life as an imposter Mafia businessman in his book *Making Jack Falcone* (2008).

A committed Mafia boss, Greg DePalma had a terrible temper and a reputation for putting the company above all other priorities. For him the Mafia "family" always came first. If your child was dying with only minutes to live, and your boss called, Mr. Garcia says, "you better leave that child and go see the boss. Because that's your real family."

To tame his very bad boss, Jack Garcia used the nonverbal principle of reciprocity known as gift giving. Anthropologists have long known that the act of accepting a material object as a gift obligates the receiver, who must reciprocate with gifts or favors of equal or greater value. Mr. Garcia gave Mr. DePalma a steady stream of gifted cigarettes, jewelry, and electronic merchandise to win his favor.

The gift-giving ploy worked well, and Garcia became like a trusted son to his boss. Of course, in this case the mock employee, Mr. Garcia, had been informing the FBI about his Mafia employer for two years. At the mobster's trial, the look on DePalma's face as Garcia testified was, in the latter's words, "classic." It was a mean, "if looks could kill" hardened stare. "He's looking at me. You know, you could tell, like, if he could just come, get his hands around my neck, you know, he'd just take me out."

DePalma was sentenced to twelve years in prison. Using a proven technique of animal trainers—repetitive goodies for good behavior—Jack Garcia successfully trained his boss. Take note, however: What's okay for FBI agents and Mafia bosses isn't okay in law-abiding offices. Gift giving to knowingly influence your employer is a bribe.

READ MY SYMBOLS

Bosses reveal a lot through the symbols they display. One boss I had was a screamer. He'd invite a senior staff member to his office and request, in a soft-spoken, world-weary voice, "Close the door." When the staffer sat down at the boss's round table, a screaming fit would erupt. He was a one-on-one screamer who yelled at captive individuals, never at groups of two or more staff. To his credit, he never screamed at junior or support people, just at directors. (I'm convinced this was not out of kindness, but just an expedient way to save energy.)

My boss's screaming fits were grating, gratuitous, and given in response to even minor matters. The first time he unleashed one of his screaming fits at me, it was because I'd indented the first line of a paragraph in a letter. "Block left! Block left!" he bellowed, waving the photocopy back and forth in his fist. "Do you think you can ignore office policy? Are you exempt? Block left!" As he screamed I watched his body bounce up and down in his chair.

For symbolism, my boss's favorite emblem was a small yellow flag bearing the image of a coiled snake. The motto beneath the rattler read, DON'T TREAD ON ME. Hung above his office door, the serpent flag was meant to strike fear in your heart as you entered the "lion's den," and I must say it worked. Just as Pavlov's dogs learned to salivate after hearing a bell, I learned to pair the rattlesnake with the boss's screaming. It took me longer to learn never to close my boss's door in the first place, and later, never to go see him at all. He'd get angry but would not, of course, yell all by himself. Nor would he come to my office and scream, since power ebbed the farther he moved from his flag.

Fortunately, not all employer emblems depict poisonous snakes. A favorite symbol of Sidney Weinberg, leader of Goldman Sachs from 1930 to 1969, was the Phi Beta Kappa key. Mr. Weinberg collected PBK keys from Brooklyn pawnshops and kept them on a wire in his desk drawer. According to veteran Sachs staffer John Whitehead, "If he had a stuffed shirt going on and on for too long about something," Weinberg "would pull the wire full of PBK keys out of his drawer and say admiringly, 'Gee, you're so awfully smart, you should have one of these'" (Peek 2008, A23).

Another former boss of mine decorated his office with officious awards; replicas and symbols of Capitol Hill; and portraits of himself standing, sitting, and posturing with powerful people. He was a reserved, usually formal person, not a screamer, and his symbols reflected the formality he expected from staff. Conspicuously on display at meetings in his office, my boss's power portraits invoked the traditional Hawaiian concept of mana. In Old Hawaii, mana was unseen spiritual power emitted by royalty. According to the Polynesian belief, crouching near a king or queen enabled you to absorb a royal dose of mana for yourself. In prehistoric Oceania, spiritual power rubbed off. For my boss, posing beside presidents made him feel powerful and "presidential" himself.

Those who hold the office of U.S. president display symbols to enhance their own perceived power. When George W. Bush was president he wore a symbolic American flag pinned to his jacket. Mr. Bush rarely left the White House without his tiny red, white, and blue patriot pin. Since its unspoken message was, "I'm more patriotic than you," Bush's staff and senior advisers wore flag lapel pins to show they were patriotic, too. Lest he seem unpatriotic, then–presidential candidate Barack Obama took to wearing the pin as well. The miniature emblem carried a sizeable measure of mana.

If leaders display lapel pins, portraits, and Phi Beta Kappa keys, their parchments also speak. A framed diploma on the wall at eye level behind a boss's desk hints at his belief that "knowledge is power." As you meet with the boss in her office, words fade after they're uttered, but diplomas keep on broadcasting, "I have the power of a college degree."

In the classic movie version of *The Wizard of Oz* (1939), the Wizard tells Scarecrow a secret about educated people: "They have one thing you haven't got: a diploma. Therefore, by virtue of the authority vested in me by the Universitartus Committiartum E Pluribus Unum, I hereby confer upon you the honorary degree of Th.D. . . . Doctor of Thinkology." But while a CEO's college degree may be cited in the annual report, you might not find a diploma on the wall.

You would not have found the certificate for a bachelor's degree in civil engineering from the University of California, for example, on President Sam W. Box's wall. Mr. Box, ex-president of Tetra Tech Inc., a worldwide provider of engineering and technical services headquartered in Pasadena, California, had no diploma because he had no degree, though he had claimed in his résumé that he did. The embarrassing lack became known after *The Wall Street Journal* made inquiries to the company for a series of investigative articles on inflated academic credentials in the workplace. For his résumé inflation, Box was demoted to vice president of Tetra in October 2008.

The *Journal* reported that "at least 10 [U.S.] senior executives and directors at publicly traded companies had corporate biographies claiming unearned academic credentials." An estimate by Kroll Inc. puts the number of employees and job applicants who exaggerate their educational credentials at about 20 percent (Tuna and Winstein 2008). For those who study business ethics, lying about a college degree or purchasing a fake degree from a diploma mill are signs of dishonesty of a serious kind.

Maurice Schweitzer, a business ethicist at the University of Pennsylvania's Wharton School, said, "I'm very concerned that if people believe you can lie and get away with it, then down the line people will start cheating on their expense reports, they'll start misrepresenting their billable hours, they'll start misusing their corporate funds" (Winstein 2008, B6). As office signals, diplomas or their absence have serious stories to tell.

CHAD'S TOXIC BOSS

Recall Richard Kelly's advice to dog owners at the beginning of this chapter. His advice applies equally well to bosses. If you give a dog a very clear and firm set of rules, and if you are consistent and reward good behavior, your dog will calm down and like you better. Treat him with consistency and he'll no longer jump up, bark at you, or bite your hand. Both your dog and your boss will benefit from a predictable daily schedule, regular personal attention—and "playing Frisbee."

In the world of wild-animal tamers, training is preceded by observation. The tamer watches his novice lion or tiger closely to determine its idiosyncrasies, habits, and moods. He then adapts his training regimen to the animal's temperament. In the business world, an anonymous manager whom I'll call "Chad" has raised the observation bar to a very high level, comparable to that of the master lion tamer Gebel-Williams.

Chad is a territory manager for a midsize technology company. It didn't take long after starting his new job for Chad to realize he was working for a classic "toxic boss." "The guy has temper tantrums, screams, uses obscenities to me on the phone, plays my colleagues off against each other, and goes into long, nonproductive tirades about customers, the industry, and members of his staff," Chad shares in an anonymous article for *BusinessWeek* (Anonymous 2008b). "I really love this job, except for my manager," he explains. "So I didn't quit. Instead I developed a formula for dealing with him."

Chad's secret formula for bosses is in perfect harmony with Kelly's advice for dog handlers. Just as a dog responds favorably to predictable feeding times, a boss responds well to predictability in his daily routine. For both man and beast, routines are psychologically "safe." Knowing breakfast is always served at 8:30 A.M., for example, a dog relaxes and calms down. Sensing that his toxic boss needed predictability as well, Chad blocked out a portion of each workday specifically to deal with him. "I set aside 8:30–10:00 A.M. every day to cater to his needs," Chad explains. As Gebel-Williams remarked about surviving in a lion cage, "You must be the same person every day." Around dangerous animals, he advised, you must be transparent.

In an office habitat, predictability includes regular personal attention. Both bosses and dogs thrive on recurrent attention from handlers. Toward this end, you may pet your dog and blow in its ear. With his boss, Chad learned that the key was regular e-mail. "I send quick e-mails throughout the day," he writes, especially during the intensive 8:30–10:00 A.M. period. "He feels no need to call me if he gets a barrage of status reports." In training, the best defense is often a good offense, and Chad's e-mail barrages worked to keep the boss safely pedestaled. From atop a circus-cage pedestal, tamers know, a lion cannot get off to a running start.

Dogs, of course, like to play Frisbee. You spin out the plastic disk-shaped toy and your dog eagerly gives chase. Something in Fido's predatory brain cannot help but go for it. A boss's "Frisbee" is not the literal toy itself, of course, but a figurative fascination with something his or her managerial mind cannot pass up. "My boss likes orders to get processed immediately," Chad writes. "So I try to process an order as soon as it arrives. If I can't get to it right away, I send him an e-mail saying that I'm wrapped up on another project. Eight out of ten times, he does the order processing for me." Take time to inventory your employer's figurative Frisbees, and spin them out for the chasing.

Like your canine pet, your boss may have two or three additional favorite toys. Unlike a dog's very tangible tennis ball and chew stick, however, your boss's favorite toy may be an intangible interest or exercise. "My boss obsesses on pricing exercises," Chad reveals in the *BusinessWeek* article. "We used to sit on the phone for hours, in what is largely a subjective process, acting like we were finding the magic price. It killed my productivity. Now, I say to my boss: 'I'm busy on Y. Would you mind working on the pricing proposal for me for Client X?' Then he's occupied for a day or so, doing what he likes to do, and he's not slowing me down." For a competitive edge, know the hidden psychology of your boss's "favorite toys."

Finally, understand your employer's monthly schedules, weekly cycles, and daily circadian rhythms. Just as dogs have "up" times when energy levels rise, and "down" times when energy wanes, bosses have better and worse periods in their job cycles. Understand the cycles to know the boss.

"My boss usually has a temper tantrum on the Monday two weeks before the end of a quarter," Chad writes. "He invariably tells me that I'm not running my territory correctly (which used to set me off). I now schedule time in my calendar to prep for this. I even tell him that he will have this tantrum before he does, and sometimes I tell him that I agree with him. It knocks him off balance" (Anonymous 2008b). Keeping big cats backed up with chair legs and off balance with whips reached into their faces is key to the lion tamer's art. With such a cyclical boss, Chad worked his tamer's magic like a pro.

If your boss is a screamer (and it seems we all have screamer stories to tell), remain perfectly calm. Since animals, including bosses, have an aversion to physical combat—even big bosses might get hurt—they resort to bluffing instead. It takes less energy and spills no blood. When threatened, puffer fish inflate, cobras extend their hoods, and dogs raise their hackles. They "enlarge" to bluff opponents away.

Your employer's yelling voice works the same way. The scream acoustically exaggerates body size to bluff you into submitting or shrinking away. It's the biological equivalent of the lion's roar. As a trainer, however, you should neither cower nor run. It's only a bluffing tactic, and your boss won't actually bite. Keep your shoulders squared toward the screamer, maintain eye contact, and stand your ground. Then say in a calm, measured voice, "There's no need to yell." Be consistent, and repeat the comment with each episode of misbehavior. If the boss's screaming can't make you cringe, cower, or back down, it will usually go away within three episodes. Keep bouncing the ball of contention back into your boss's court. Through your calm actions and words you seem to be saying, "If you really want to fight, then come on. But stop the bluffing act—it's not working for you."

STEVE'S DISAPPEARING BOSS

The defining sign of a "disappeared" boss is an empty office. In stressful times at work, a CEO's vacated space signals a leadership vacuum in the firm. On condition of anonymity, Steve, a program director at a national association, recounted his experience with an absentee boss. "My boss arrived each morning at 9:00 A.M.," he explained. Carrying a pair of leather briefcases stuffed with file folders he'd taken home the night before, Steve's boss would stroll into his office, sit behind his dark maple desk, and toil diligently until 5:00 P.M. The boss's workday was always the same, 9:00 to 5:00, "as fixed as the daily routine of a fence lizard."

"I should say *almost* always the same," Steve corrected, "since at certain times of the year my boss's office would be dark with nobody behind the desk. My boss was out but not out on vacation."

"'Where's Mike?' I asked. 'Out of town at a meeting,' his secretary told me. 'He can't be,' I told her. 'It's crunch time around here, a week before the big meeting!' Since our big meeting drew people from around the world, the week before was crazy with details and last-minute changes."

As I listened to Steve's story about Mike's serial disappearances, I detected a pattern. Mike's office would go predictably dark a week in advance of critical events. An upcoming meeting of the board of directors would frighten him away. When the going got tough in Steve's office, his boss flew away to an irrelevant meeting in Seattle, Phoenix, or Atlanta. Anywhere far away would do. Like *Catch-22*'s fictional Major Major—the commander who sneaked out his office's back window when visitors came—Mike was conveniently out when he should have been in.

When office tension peaked, Steve's leader flew the coop. Mike would go to a big-city destination, attend a daytime meeting, and go out at night. Since Steve signed the company checks, he saw the receipts Mike had submitted for expenses and learned that his boss had been out singing in piano bars! When the association's board learned of the problem, through Steve, Mike's days were numbered. Caught in his disappearing act, Mike stepped down and disappeared for good.

Disappearing boss syndrome, or DBS, has many guises, but the message is the same. When corporate heat turns up, the boss vacates and no one sits in the CEO's chair. Rome may burn, but that office stays empty. DBS made news in a celebrated case in Manhattan during the summer of 2007. Tensions grew over the fate of hedge funds at Bear Stearns Companies in New York, as more than a billion dollars went down the drain. At this critical juncture, Bear Stearns CEO James Cayne, seventy-three, materially disappeared from his corporate office. First, Mr. Cayne fled to a private New Jersey golf course. "The golf course for him was an escape," John Angelo, a frequent golf partner, told *The Wall Street Journal* (Anonymous 2007d). Later, Cayne disappeared to a ten-day bridge tournament in Nashville, Tennessee. Finally, after Bear Stearns hedge funds lost $1.6 billion, Cayne disappeared from his office permanently and stepped down as CEO. For his absenteeism under fire, the editors of *Fortune* magazine ranked Cayne number 30 in its "101 Dumbest Moments in Business" for 2007, and on May 30, 2008, Bear Stearns went out of business.

DBS is an acute reaction controlled by the brain's fight-or-flight response. In the 1920s physiologist Walter B. Cannon identified the sympathetic nervous system's *emergency reaction,* which prepared the body to exert high levels of physical energy to either fight or flee. The fight-or-flight response is coordinated by central command neurons in the hypothalamus and brain stem. Faced with tough business problems, an angry boss will stay in the office and fight. A fearful boss will physically leave the office and take flight. In the above cases each boss let his body do the talking. Stepping away left visibly empty desks that spoke of corporate neglect, and flight itself became the sign.

For the animal brain the purpose of flight is to escape capture. Chameleons flee through the visual channel, changing color to blend into the background and disappear. Rabbits sit perfectly still to keep predators from seeing them, or run away and disappear to another location. Bosses escape to golf courses, bridge tournaments, and piano bars, but eventually must return to the office and the fate awaiting them there. More than most, the well-publicized case of James Cayne shows how visible being absent can be.

Does Your Boss . . .

(1) **Sleep overnight in the office?** It could be a sign of marital discord. In 2008, Zong Qinghou, founder of the Wahaha Group Company—China's largest soft-drink empire—sometimes slept in his corporate office to avoid arguments with his wife and daughter about problems the company faced with rival Groupe Danone SA of France.

(2) **Hold meetings outside the office on a balcony?** This could be a sign of corporate strife. On July 23, 2008, Robert Dudley was quoted in *The Wall Street Journal* as saying, "I spend a lot of

time holding meetings out on the balcony of my office" (White 2008). Mr. Dudley, who was chief executive of Russia's TNK-BP Ltd., feared eavesdropping by rival Russian shareholders who wanted him out of the country.

(3) Avoid e-mail, use different telephone numbers, and return calls only from moving vehicles? This, too, may be a sign of office eavesdropping. To prevent spying in 2008, Brazilian banker Daniel Dantas of Rio de Janeiro turned off the TV and removed batteries from his cell phones before an interview at his Opportunity investment company headquarters. His habit of eschewing e-mail and making phone calls outside his office came in response to widespread fear that the Brazilian government was "always listening."

(4) Shout and pound the table? This could signal a pugnacious boss capable of inciting boardroom brawls. When he took over as head of Beatrice Foods Company in 1976, Wallace N. Rasmussen worked to replace all of his board's outside directors with new faces. Asked how his wife and family coped with the boss's twenty-hour workdays, Mr. Rasmussen reportedly replied that they should be gotten rid of if they get in the way.

(5) Hem and haw when asked hard questions? "Hemming" (speech hesitations) and "hawing" (fumbling for words) are nonverbal signs of deception. Brought on by stress, the throat tightens and words don't easily flow. On October 6, 2008, Richard Fuld, Jr., CEO of Lehman Brothers Holdings Inc., testified before a U.S. House committee that he had not deceived investors about the economic health of his firm prior to its collapse on Wall Street. According to *The Wall Street Journal*, Mr. Fuld testified "in sometimes halting language" (Craig 2008a, A3).

BEHIND STEEL GATES

"They're behind steel gates," David Perry told Sarah Needleman (Needleman 2008). An executive job recruiter, Mr. Perry learned that CEOs and other high-level executives often disappear and keep themselves reclusively out of public view. They may not answer phone calls, letters, or e-mails, and behave as if they're not really there at all. The secrecy of their whereabouts and their unwillingness to come out—a bit like Boo Radley in the novel *To Kill a Mockingbird* (1960)—can make the job of a headhunter challenging.

David Perry, however, is determinedly up to the challenge. To find and meet reclusive bosses, Mr. Perry plays Sherlock Holmes and hunts for clues about how the bosses behave, where they dine, and even where they bathe. The clues he collects tell him where to track down prospects who periodically exit from behind their steel gates.

In one of Perry's cases a secret phone number turned out to be the key. His assignment to track down the CEO of a New York technology firm failed when he used regular communication channels. Indeed, Mr. Perry, whose Perry-Martel International office is located in Ottawa, Canada, came up empty-handed time after time. The CEO disappeared through a tactic of serially unanswered phone calls.

Not to be outdone, David flew to New York and stealthily visited the basement of the firm's headquarters. There he handed a janitor a hundred dollars and a self-addressed envelope in which to mail the CEO's secret telephone number, on the theory that the big boss had a private washroom, with a phone, somewhere in the building.

Soon after, when the telephone number arrived, Perry knew he had his CEO. He called and offered the prospect a new position with a large software firm. When the elusive executive agreed to take the job, a deal was made. Had Perry not searched for hidden clues behind the steel gate, there would have been no deal.

Like lions, tigers, and bears (and, of course, dogs), CEOs exhibit fixed behavior patterns and predictable routines. Understanding their hunting and feeding habits, knowing how they mark their dens, and learning how they behave when cornered will help you survive on the corporate veldt. The more you know about the animal nature of your boss's brain, the better you'll be able to manage that creature and get along. Getting along is, in fact, our topic in the next chapter, "Signs of Office Rapport."

TWELVE

Signs of Office Rapport

A study by the Center for Creative Leadership
in Greensboro, N.C., with Manchester Partners
International, found that 40 percent of management
hires fail, and the key reason for the turnover
(82 percent) is their inability to build good relationships
with peers and subordinates.

—*The San Diego Union-Tribune* (Anonymous, 1998)

The best offices find tangible ways to build rapport with colleagues. Recall from chapter 9 the offices of Decagon Devices in Pullman, Washington, where employees are encouraged to socialize on breaks over soccer games and Ping-Pong. When you play sports with colleagues—kick balls to teammates, return your opponent's serves, keep a scorecard—you build trust and foster rapport. Back at the workplace, you find that information flows more easily through informal channels that crosscut the vertical lines of your firm's organization chart. The freer, horizontal exchange of information promotes creativity and enhances efficiency on the job.

You can see office rapport—or detect its absence—in nonverbal cues of exchange. As I've noted, staffers who like one another tend to eat together, trade food items, exchange family photos, and share personal details about their office décor. In the hospital administration office I observed at a place I'll call Mercy Medical Center, in Washington State, I noted countless exchanges of small favors unrelated to work. Rapport was good, and staffers freely shared the information they needed to do their jobs.

There was one exception, however, to the reciprocity rule. Karen, age sixty, rarely shared in office exchanges. She never joined colleagues for lunch in the cafeteria, but instead ate meals alone in her cubicle. No candy or cookies changed hands, no family photos were given or received, no tour of her cubicle's knickknacks was given or proffered. As one of Karen's co-workers told me, "The keepsakes in her workspace are total mysteries. She's never shared anything with any of us. Karen's personal life is a blank. There's a framed photo of a man on her wall, but we don't know who he is."

In Karen's case, there was no give at the office and next to no take. When she left work at 3:30 P.M., Karen waited until she had walked past colleagues before saying good-bye. She timed her words so only the back of her head showed.

Karen's lack of office rapport came with a price tag. Since there was no informal conduit to colleagues, she failed to communicate work-related details they needed to hear. While co-workers were at lunch Karen would leave file folders on their desktops without the courtesy of telling them why. A co-worker would return from break to find a phone number on a sticky note posted to her screen, again with no explanation. *Please call,* Karen's note would say, without a word about who had called. Karen wouldn't reveal how many new doctors were accepted to practice at the hospital, making it hard for her colleagues to arrange for physician orientations. Since the rapport channel linking Karen to office mates was sealed off, necessary information didn't flow.

How might Karen's rapport problem be turned around? Rather than bring the issue to her attention consciously in words—which had been tried, unsuccessfully, several times—I'd propose a nonverbal solution that would speak to Karen's emotions. I would bring her into the loop at the next staff meeting with a morale-booster I call Photo Share, in which I ask staff to bring two photographs from home to share at the monthly meeting. The brief sharing exercise would be billed as a way to get to know the person behind the job.

By sharing photos—personal images of pets, home remodels, vacations, grandchildren, and so on—staff can get a glimpse of what goes on in their colleagues' lives apart from work. As an exercise, Photo Share mimics the natural exchange of small favors that leads to office rapport. By sharing photographs, Karen would likely reenter the rapport network. Exchanging nonverbal pictures of home life and loved ones would send a powerfully personal message about "who *we* are."

CREATIVITY BOOSTER

Michael Kinsley's closet-size modular workspace, adjustable desk, and computer docking station were exactly like those everyone else had. On the grassy campus of Microsoft headquarters in Redmond, Washington, the buildings, equipment, and workers— staffers who were mostly young and free-spirited—looked much the same. Indeed, the look and feel of sameness permeated Microsoft's tree-lined, glass-walled workplace.

Mr. Kinsley, former *National Review* editor and cohost of CNN's TV talk show *Crossfire,* came to Washington State from Washington, D.C., to develop Microsoft's new electronic magazine, *Slate.* "I had no business plan, no staff, no anything," Kinsley said. "All I had was an office" (Auletta 1996).

Though eleven years older than the average age of his nine-thousand Redmond colleagues, forty-five-year-old Michael Kinsley fit right in. This was partly due to his nondescript, casual dress style and mildly eccentric body language. The corporate culture at Microsoft is nothing if not a bit quirky and generally tolerant of

nerdlike deportment, clothing, and worldview. Following Microsoft's custom of eschewing jackets and ties in favor of jeans and a
natural look, Kinsley wore neutral-colored L.L.Bean khakis, open-
collar cotton shirts, nerdy white socks, and academic glasses with
clear-plastic frames. Since he held his arms down close to his sides,
few hand gestures were visible when he talked. In conversation his
voice was deliberate and soft-spoken. Unblinking eyes stared out
through round-framed spectacles and locked on to colleagues faces
(Auletta 1996).

Designing an online magazine from scratch was both challenging and frustrating. Yet as Michael Kinsley toiled each day in
his Washington State office, ensconced in Microsoft's modular
Building 25, he was happy with his decision to leave Washington,
D.C. As Ken Auletta wrote in a *New Yorker* article describing Mr.
Kinsley's venture, one of the things Michael enjoyed most about
his Microsoft office was its "easy rapport."

Rapport is a pleasant feeling of mutual trust, affinity, and friendship established through verbal and nonverbal means. The English
word "rapport" derives from Old French ("to bring back") via Latin
("to carry"), from the seven-thousand-year-old Indo-European
root word *per-,* "fellow traveler." As fellow travelers, Michael Kinsley and his colleagues in Building 25 got along well. Trekking
with co-workers in hallways, along sidewalks, and to and from the
company-subsidized cafeteria helped them see eye-to-eye. Walking together, we will see, holds a key to rapport.

Thus it was that Mr. Kinsley's newborn *Slate* magazine, incu-
bated in the climate of good rapport at Microsoft, successfully
launched in 1996, won a National Magazine Award for content,
and became a respected brand name in journalism. *Slate* pio-
neered the use of hyperlinks and blogs in electronic publications.
On December 21, 2004, *Slate* was sold to the Washington Post
Company, where it remains to this day, for between $15 and $20
million. Subsequently, Michael Kinsley left *Slate* to become the

editorial page editor at the *Los Angeles Times*. Without the rapport
he'd enjoyed in his Microsoft office, it's hard to imagine that *Slate*
would have become a success. Rapport paved the way for the cooperation, agreement, and teamwork that was required for him to
launch his new venture and get the job done.

Inside the office, we can build rapport through nonverbal channels. These include the tactile channel for touch, the visual channel for gesture, and the auditory channel for sound. Chief among
Michael Kinsley's rapport-building pathways at Microsoft was
his trademark soft tone of voice. Spoken words have both an ob-
jective dictionary sense and a more subjective sense in their mode
of delivery. The way words sound can be as meaningful as what they
say. *Voice quality,* the way in which a verbal statement is presented—
its rhythm, prosody, breathiness, hoarseness, softness, or loudness;
its scolding, serious, or sarcastic tone—conveys emotion, feeling,
and mood.

Outside the office, in the wild kingdom, the more aggressive
an animal becomes the louder, lower, and harsher its voice will
sound. A case in point is the mountain gorilla (*Gorilla gorilla berengei*).
Its harsh, roaring screams rend the air to make a male gorilla's
350-pound body seem bigger still. Among human beings, while a
deep, resonant voice in the office may sound dominant and betoken high status, its threatening overtones can hurt rapport. I remember the painfully loud voice of one of my former colleagues,
Josh, as he bellowed at staff meetings in our company conference
room. Josh had a nasty habit of emitting explosive throat-clearing
noises to interrupt staffers he disagreed with. Though he was
friendly one-on-one, his overloud meeting voice damaged rapport and made him one of the least-liked people in the office.

According to Eugene Morton of the National Zoological Park
in Washington, D.C., mammalian sounds are blends of three basic vocalizations: growls, barks, and whines. Josh's conference-
room voice echoed Morton's three modes as he variously spoke in

low-pitched raspy, overloud staccato, and high-pitched whiney voice tones to argue with us over the most minor details. In contrast to Josh, Michael Kinsley used a consistently soft-spoken voice with the right "rapport appeal" to win friends and influence people at Microsoft.

Subject to cultural shaping, voice qualities are universal across cultures. Adults everywhere use a softer, higher-pitched voice to speak to infants and young children. The soft voice quality is innately friendly and suggests a posture of nonaggressiveness and parental care. With each other, men and women around the world use a light voice in friendly greetings and in courtship to say, "I care." And loud voices are almost universally disliked. In the office, the number-one complaint is about colleagues who use loud voices on the telephone. In the close confines of an eight-hour day, an overloud voice has a cumulative effect guaranteed to spoil rapport.

It is a truism of body language that seemingly minor details of dress and demeanor carry major meanings. And indeed, rapport may hinge on a trifle. Consider the design of a colleague's eyeglasses. How we feel about co-workers can be subtly influenced by the roundness or angularity of their frames. The glasses Michael Kinsley wore at Microsoft were rounded and nonthreatening, making him seem easy to approach. A man wearing round, goggle-eyed spectacles is not likely to bite you. Kinsley looked more like an affable fish than a hungry shark.

In a 1999 corporate photo of Mr. Kinsley, seated at his Building 25 desk, he has on a friendly, pale blue striped shirt with an unbuttoned collar exposing the harmless white neckline of his T-shirt. Kinsley's big rounded lenses bring fishbowls to mind. His magnified eyes seem to lure you in for a closer look. The circular, clear plastic frames also pick up the roundness of his face and accent the curvilinear shape of his forehead. Michael Kinsley's round glasses and oval face send a message of easy rapport: "You can come closer—I won't bite."

The rounded features associated with women's and children's faces and bodies appeal to us as friendly cues. Smooth, rounded shoulders, foreheads, and glasses say, "Approach me." On the other hand, the angular, craggy features associated with men's faces, squared shoulders, and generally rectangular glasses subtly warn us to keep our distance. In an office such cues broadcast continuously throughout the workday. The friendly effect of roundness and the more intimidating effect of angularity work subliminally to enhance or discourage rapport.

Rapport Interrupted

When a boss with whom you've had easy rapport gives you the cold shoulder—avoids casual interaction with you—heed the sign. A sudden change in rapport means you could be laid off. Marcia Finberg, vice president of marketing at a hospital complex in Phoenix, Arizona, knew there was a problem when the hospital CEO she'd always made sociable small talk with suddenly avoided her. Ms. Finberg noticed that when she approached him he gave responses that were succinct and vocally cold (Mattioli 2008, D6).

"Cold shoulder" is a figurative phrase for turning away and being unfriendly. In the literal body-language sense of cold shoulder, you see someone who rotates his face and torso around to show

When the boss wanted to cut off rapport, a shoulder did the talking.

you the side of his upper arm. Seeing an arm's deltoid muscle instead of the person's face is a sobering sign. It's the impersonal cold shoulder suggesting you're no longer on his or her "A-list."

Marcia Finberg's foreboding, an intuition based on her boss's changed demeanor and avoidant body language, came true three months later when her position was cut and she was let go. Finberg was perceptive in seeing that her cold-shoulder treatment was actually a defense mechanism. The boss wasn't avoiding her personally, but rather avoiding the conflict that a face-to-face meeting might incur. "Bosses," Judith Glaser of New York's Benchmark Communications Inc. says, "are particularly conflict-averse" (Mattioli 2008, D6). When Ms. Finberg's boss wanted to terminate rapport, he let his shoulder do the talking.

ON WALKABOUT

Industrial psychologists encourage us to talk about our problems in the workplace. In group-psychology sessions talk is therapeutic. As an anthropologist who studies office culture, I propose that we also "walk about" our problems. Consider a mini–case study I conducted as a participant-observer at one of my former offices:

Jan and I had worked for the same firm in the same office building for months, but I confess I didn't like her. You could say we had no rapport. All of the nonverbal elements were missing, so rapport itself—the pleasant feeling of mutual trust—was missing as well.

In her abrupt and aggressive mode—chin up and out, shoulders back—Jan would pop into my office and ask in a demanding, over-loud voice that I get my monthly report to her "right away." Jan was pushy in a most unfriendly way. She clomped when she walked; gave impatient, palm-down beating gestures; and punched her computer keyboard hard enough to shake the monitor.

Since I didn't like Jan's bedside manner, instead of handing over my report I'd stall. Jan would come back the next day and repeat her demand with lowered eyebrows and a sterner glare. I'd stall again. On the third day Jan's boss would stop by to ask for the report. Since I had rapport with him, I'd send in the document but know Jan would be coming by for next month's report, and the one after that.

Come to think of it, our rapport was subzero. It went on for months with repeat episodes of clomping, tense lips, lowered brows, and loud voice—and my passive-aggressive stall.

But something finally happened to break the cycle. We flew on the same United Airlines flight to a business meeting in San Francisco. Though we didn't sit together, we deplaned together and exchanged a greeting in the Jetway. After flying all day with strangers, it's nice to see someone familiar, even someone you don't necessarily like.

What happened next caught me by surprise. We walked in tandem side-by-side, step for step up the Jetway to the gate, then walked a quarter mile together on to the baggage claim. What surprised me was that by the time we picked up our baggage from the carrousel, we'd also picked up rapport. Something about the physical act of walking together had brought us emotionally closer after months of standing apart.

Recall the seven-thousand-year-old meaning of the word "rapport": "fellow traveler." When Jan and I walked together at the airport we became fellow travelers. We shared the walkways, stepped in the same direction toward a common goal, saw the same sights en route, and arrived at the same destination. Going on airport walkabout had bonded us within minutes as we'd not bonded in the office for months. When we got to our hotel we had a drink together at the bar, and for the first time ever had a decent conversation. From that day forward, Jan and I ceased to be foes. She never again scowled or stomped into my office, and I never again stalled. Nonverbally, thanks to our communal stroll, we were an affable twosome.

The Merits of a Good Walkabout

Mr. Guboo Ted Thomas, the last initiated elder of the Yuin tribe of Australia's fabled South Coast, worked out of his Melbourne office at the Australian Institute of Aboriginal Studies. His territory, the mountainous coastal region of New South Wales, was both vast and majestic. Guboo—which means "your good friend" in the Yuin language—spent a good deal of time out of his office in the beautiful, forested backcountry going on walkabout with politicians and conservationists.

Guboo was born under a gum tree in the small town of Braidwood, just east of Canberra, in 1909. When Guboo was nine, relatives took him on walkabout from Mallacoota, near the border of Victoria, to the Hawkesbury River, just north of Sydney, to teach him about mountains, rock formations, rivers, and the other sacred sites of his Aborigine kin. As they walked together step for step through open countryside, Guboo learned the sacred Dreamtime stories, songs, and lore of his ancestral landscape. The land became his textbook, which he studied by looking and listening rather than reading.

After a long career as a fisherman, Guboo became a tribal elder himself, and dedicated his final years to preserving Aborigine Dreamtime sites. The *Sydney Morning Herald,* which described Guboo as "a clever and wily negotiator," reported that he convinced the New South Wales government to set aside substantial tracts of real estate as national parks to preserve the land. He accomplished his goals by asking eloquently in words, and by taking officials on even more eloquent walkabouts to the places he wished to protect.

Guboo could have stayed in his office and written letters from the Institute. But he chose to act instead. The steps he took toward preservation were literal steps. He went on walkabout. Sharing the walkabout made colleagues fellow travelers in his quest.

In 1979 the Australian state of New South Wales ordered that logging cease on Guboo's favorite mountain, Mumbulla. "His work with the Institute of Aboriginal Studies was groundbreaking," the *Sydney Morning Herald* wrote, "and became the basis of all future land claims along the South Coast" (Newstead 2002). For Guboo, walking with others toward a common goal paid off.

The Better Business of Walking Together

Recall from chapter 10 that sitting is the preferred posture of our primate relatives, the monkeys and apes. We human primates who work in offices spend a good deal of time seated, as our fingers do the walking on keyboards. As natural as being seated is, the best path to rapport, as we've seen, is not sitting but strolling. A bipedal stride enabled our earliest ancestors 3 million years ago to cover great distances across African savannah grasslands. Survival required that they stay continually on the move, and daily walking together bonded them as allies.

The earliest physical evidence for human-style walking dates back 3.5 million years to the tracks of three upright ancients who strolled across a bed of fresh volcanic ash one day in East Africa, in what is now Laetoli, Tanzania. The footprints are nearly identical to those of modern humans. The ancient ones likely knew each other as family and kin.

"I am in the moment, living the experience, when I am walking," a modern human, Joy Jones, told *The Washington Post* (Jones 1992). In the office world today, walking promotes feelings of being in the moment, and more. Walking to lunch with a colleague enables you to share the bipedal experience, which not only has the syncopated beat and two-point rhythm of music but also the oscillating movements of dance. En route together you share the footpath, see the same landmarks you both pass by, and anticipate a shared destination where you'll enjoy food and drink together. The simple act of walking to a lunch spot with an office mate promotes conversation and easy rapport.

The rhythm of walking clears the mind for thinking. Many philosophers were lifetime walkers who found that bipedal rhythms facilitated creative contemplation and thought. Followers of Aristotle (384–322 B.C.), for example, were known as Peripatetics because they walked and underwent "restless practices" as they thought and shared ideas, rather than merely sitting in place. In his short life Henry David Thoreau (1817–1862), who pondered the meaning of human life in natural environments, walked an estimated 250,000 miles—ten times the circumference of Earth.

Though we manage to sit for hours in office chairs, we are wired with powerful instincts to move. Our legs originated 400 million years ago from the lobe fins of Devonian fishes. As babies, we begin advancing one limb at a time on all fours between the sixth and ninth month of life, crawling for the sheer pleasure of movement. We are born with two walking reflexes. The *plantar reflex* causes our lower limbs to contract extensor muscles when our feet touch a horizontal surface. Held under the arms, a baby can support its own weight and take several steps forward on the floor. When a baby's leg touches the side of a flat surface like the vertical riser of a stair step, the *placing reflex* automatically lifts the baby's leg and places its foot on the horizontal plane.

Since we are natural wanderers—and since daily confinement in offices feels unnatural—it's not surprising that our species invented ways to conduct business out of doors. We meet, memo, e-mail, and text-message each other indoors, but a great deal of business also takes place outdoors, in bipedal mode at getaway retreats, resorts, and other "natural" places that cater to our innate need for walking. Chief among these latter-day grasslands are golf courses.

THE BETTER BUSINESS OF GOLF

What makes golf such an integral part of today's business world? In France deals are made at Parc du Golf in the heart of the major business district Aix les Milles. In Japan golf has become an essential tool for younger workers who play to adapt to their new company's corporate culture. In the United States, according to *Golf Magazine*, 98 percent of CEOs play golf. There's something decidedly business-friendly about the game. As we'll see, it's not just the score that matters but the setting. Golf provides an evolutionary correct landscape for corporate walkabout and rapport.

"You need clubs and balls in your bag for golf. Bring other tools to conduct business," writes Ben Miller in his article for *Puget Sound Business Journal*, "Business Golf Has Little to Do with Putting" (Miller 2005). It seems the score doesn't matter as much as the bipedal blueprint of the game. Miller shares an opinion from Ms. Patty Pearcy, then a controller at Seattle Pacific Industries: "[Golf] has helped me network. It is becoming a requirement, like an M.B.A. A lot of relationships are built outside the office."

Originally known as *colf*, golf was played in Holland from at least the year A.D. 1297 with balls made of fine-grained hardwoods such as elm, box, and beech. In 1848 a superior ball was made from tree sap, a rubbery substance known as gutta-percha, which was boiled and shaped in iron molds.

Nonverbally, golf reconnects players to their ancestral tree-climbing lives and savannah-grassland experiences—what our nomadic forebears originally knew in East Africa—and to their hunter-gatherer roots. Golfers focus incredible attention on gripping the club, which in shape and thickness resembles a tree limb. Blending power and precision grips, players strike balls as if swatting small prey animals on the turf.

The basic body movements of golf—gripping, arm swinging, body bending, and striding—are embedded in primeval motor centers of our brain. Golfing is an evolutionary correct way to rekindle the savannah-grassland experiences our nomadic ancestors once enjoyed. Today's game is enjoyed by small, face-to-face bands of players who wander through artificial grasslands in pursuit of spherical prey, dimpled white balls, which they strike with high-tech branch substitutes called clubs. The English word "club" derives from Old Norse *klubba,* "heavy stick weapon."

In the career realm, important deals are nurtured on golf courses. Stalking through grassy fields in close-knit, face-to-face groups, sticks in hand—hunting for game balls and walloping them—businesspeople enjoy the same concentration, competition, and camaraderie their ancestors once experienced in Africa. No gas station, subway, or billboard signs disturb the "natural" view. It's a setting not for commerce but for camaraderie.

A Walk on the Grass

Twenty million years ago in the Miocene epoch, parts of East Africa changed from rain forest to open woodlands as our arboreal ancestors began living a part of their lives on the ground. Two million years ago in the Pleistocene epoch, the first humans (genus *Homo*) lived in eastern Africa as hunter-gatherers on tropical, shrubby grasslands—in hot, flat, open countryside with scattered trees and little shade known as savannahs (from the Taino word *zabana,* "flat grassland").

Early humans would feel right at home strolling the eighth hole at Pebble Beach in California, with its cliffs, boulders, surf, and tree-lined hills spanning the horizon. The fairway resembles a game trail, the sand traps could be dried salt ponds, and neither office buildings nor power poles disturb the natural view.

The very names of golf courses suggest we perceive them as natural habitats. The best-rated U.S. public course, Brown Deer Park in Milwaukee, Wisconsin, is named after the most-hunted U.S. game

animal, the deer. The best-rated private course, Cypress Point
Club at Pebble Beach in California, is named after a tree. Hell's
Half Acre, reputedly the world's largest sand trap, is located in
New Jersey on the seventh hole of a course named Pine Valley.

Because the savannah experience took place during a critical
time in human evolution—as *Homo*'s brain was expanding faster
than any brain in the history of vertebrates—grassland habitats
left an indelible mark on the species. Today we remodel earth to
our liking by flattening and smoothing its surface to idealize the
original plains upon which our ancestors hunted, gathered, and
camped. We find psychic comfort in semiopen spaces, and "Neo-
savannah Grassland," with its scattered bushes and reassuring
clumps of trees, is the landscaping theme of college campuses, city
parks, and cemeteries, and of the golf courses where we do business
away from the office.

RAPPORT MEANS GOING AND DOING TOGETHER

In its deepest sense, rapport is about doing things together. In the
workplace it comes about through shared activities, as when co-
workers play Ping-Pong or kick soccer balls together on break. With
its physical give and take, the shared activity engenders feelings of
togetherness, which play a valuable role in effective workplaces.

You have seen how the physical activity of walking together—
whether along a corporate walkway to Microsoft's cafeteria or
along a grassy fairway in France's Parc du Golf—leads naturally to
business relationships. The very rhythm of walking works to unite
those who share its gait. To unite with colleagues in the workplace,
you don't need a team-building course. Just get together and go on
walkabout.

In the next chapter we will go a bit further beyond simple rapport and learn about trust and the ways it's made evident. On the
job, what exactly does trust look like?

THIRTEEN

The Tokens of Trust

**It takes years to build up trust,
and only seconds to destroy it.**

Y ou can learn more about a company from its nonverbal signs, signals, and cues than you can from its official pronouncements. The carefully chosen words of a company's annual report may tell you less about the firm than, say, where its president parks his car. Consider the case of Herbert "Bart" McDade III, former president of Lehman Brothers Holdings Inc. His peculiar parking place may have signaled quite a lot about the financial condition of Lehman Brothers.

"Dear Shareholders and Clients," Mr. McDade's company wrote in its annual report. "In 2007, Lehman Brothers produced another year of record net revenues, net income, and earnings per share and successfully managed through the difficult market environment. Our global platform of diversified businesses also produced record performance across each of our business segments as well as in Europe and Asia" (Lehman Brothers 2007).

These are encouraging words. But a year later, on September 15, 2008, Lehman Brothers filed for Chapter 11 bankruptcy. At the time it was the largest bankruptcy in U.S. history. On that fateful Monday, glum, angry, and shocked office workers filed out of the flashy Lehman Brothers building near New York's Times Square. They carried cardboard boxes filled with personal belongings and walked out the front door, forever. The record revenues, income, and earnings written about in the 2007 report suddenly seemed unreal.

If the 2007 shareholders statement said, "All is well at Lehman," Bart McDade's parking habits said otherwise. "When financial markets were rising," *The Wall Street Journal* reported, "McDade out of superstition repeatedly parked his car in the same spot behind Lehman's headquarters in Manhattan" (Craig 2008a, C1). The article went on to say that McDade, who trusts in the ancient Taoist belief of feng shui, turned down one office for another that had "better energy."

It may seem odd that a banker responsible for handling billions of dollars in assets would be so superstitious. A superstition is a belief or practice that is irrationally maintained through ignorance or in spite of knowledge of the laws of nature. Parking one's car in the same magical spot to keep markets rising is akin to carrying a rabbit's foot for good luck. In a banker, neither habit inspires trust.

We begin our look at trust signals with Lehman Brothers Holdings because its example illustrates just how fragile trust can be, and how quickly it can vanish. When you don't have trust in management, especially in a seriously stumbling economy, it may be time to consider your options. In the Lehman case visible tokens of trust had all but vanished as the world economic crisis deepened in 2008.

Founded in 1850, Lehman Brothers grew to become a global financial services firm with $230 billion in assets and more than twenty-eight thousand employees. Headquartered in New York City, the company had regional offices in London, Tokyo, and elsewhere around the world.

The Feel of Trust

"Trust" is a firm reliance on the integrity, ability, or character of a person, animal, or thing. The English word "trust" has ancient roots and derives from the seven-thousand-year-old Indo-European root word *deru-*, which means to be firm, solid, and steadfast. *Deru-* also has specialized senses of "wood," "tree," and derivatives referring to objects made of wood. There's a strong sense of solidity to the word.

As primates with grasping digits, we derive a sense of animal reassurance from the solid objects we hold in our hands. When we climbed trees as children, we trusted the limbs we held on to would not let us down. As working adults, we like to feel that our colleagues will be similarly firm and solid on our behalf. Trust on the job is something we literally need to feel.

In the company's 2007 annual report, President McDade's boss, Chairman and CEO Richard Fuld, Jr., is pictured standing in his office overlooking the Manhattan skyline. He wears a dark suit, a pressed white shirt, and a knotted salmon-colored tie. His right hand is placed deeply inside his pants pocket, while his open, seemingly relaxed left hand dangles by his side. Not known for an easy grin, Mr. Fuld smiles for the camera. If Fuld, a weightlifter, looks wholly in charge, it is due mainly to his muscular build, piercing gaze, and perfectly level head. That he's secure in his habitat clearly shows.

As reported in *Fortune* magazine, Richard Fuld's athletic body and "notorious temper" earned him the nickname "Gorilla." *Mother Jones* magazine attributed the nickname to Fuld's "imposing presence and pugilistic style." He reportedly once got into a fight with another parent at his son's hockey game. At Lehman Brothers, Mr. Fuld was known for his aggressive management style. A Lehman colleague remarked that Fuld once grabbed him by the arms and threatened to fire him.

In the context of banking, neither Bart McDade's superstition nor his boss's pugilistic temperament inspired trust. Both outlooks, after all, are contrary to reason, and both are out of character for bankers. Some have suggested that Richard Fuld's fatal flaw may have been his hubris, the tendency to respond to events with arrogance and overbearing pride. As Christian Plumb and Dan Wilchins point out in their analysis for Reuters, "At key junctures Fuld seems to have played a game of brinksmanship, refusing to accept offers that could have rescued the firm because they didn't reflect the value he saw in the bank" (Plumb and Wilchins 2008).

As CEO Fuld assertively stood his ground in the 2007 office photo, he gave no ground to buyers who might have rescued his ailing firm. The belief that his company was worth more than it actually was led the Gorilla to stand pat—and then to suddenly declare bankruptcy in 2008. Like a silverback male, Dick Fuld was a man not easily moved. He felt Lehman Brothers should command a higher purchase price, and stubbornly clung to that belief.

For bankers who deal in large sums of money, superstition and hubris are discouraging signs. Since it shows a disregard for reason and scientific law, superstition is an especially troubling signal. Yet both Mr. McDade and Mr. Fuld appeared to be fervently superstitious about one of Lehman Brothers' key financial products. As the U.S. housing market peaked in early 2005, Lehman Brothers invested billions of dollars in home mortgages, which the company then repackaged as "collateralized debt obligations," or CDOs, which were sold to other investors as securities.

The English word "security" means freedom from risk or danger. Though CDOs are called securities, they are anything but secure. So complex are the mathematical formulas for CDOs that nobody can offer a reasonable explanation of their value or of how they actually work. But when reason fails in financial markets, superstition comes to the fore and bankers need only believe. Lehman aggressively cobbled together and sold CDOs, and even counted them as "assets" on its balance sheets. In effect, CDOs had become magical pieces of paper with awesome powers. Printed on parchment to give them a more substantial feel, they were pronounced "real" by Lehman's corporate sense of touch.

When U.S. housing prices declined in 2006, and subprime mortgage holders began to default on their loans, CDOs quickly lost value. The parchments themselves seemed less magical and felt a lot less real. Public trust in their power as assets all but evaporated. CEO Fuld, however, superstitiously clung to his belief that Lehman's mortgage-backed securities were solid. Clearly, all was not well at Lehman Brothers, but Mr. Fuld believed the company had enough capital to make it through the crunch. As an anthropologist, I would say he seemed to think the magical pieces of paper would save him.

It was not to be, of course. Richard Fuld's belief in those documents—subprime mortgage certificates and CDOs—was little more than superstition. After Fuld's buyout deals with Bank of America and Barclays Capital failed, Fuld hastily took Lehman Brothers to court and declared bankruptcy on the fateful September morning in 2008. Public trust in the firm and its pugilistic CEO would go bankrupt as well. "Mr. Fuld's decisions drove the company toward ruin, as his board stood idly by," said New York State comptroller Thomas DiNapoli (Tong 2008). Nobody in the Lehman boardroom, it seemed, dared to take on the eight-hundred-pound gorilla in the room.

A Saxophone and a Bomber Jacket

As a legitimate businessman, Norman Hsu was woefully unsuccessful. But as a builder of trust, the soft-spoken wheeler-dealer from Hong Kong was something of a genius. As a result of favors he did for then-Senator Hillary Clinton, like raising more than $800,000 for her run for the office of U.S. president, she publicly called Mr. Hsu "a trusted friend" (Dugan et al. 2007, A14).

"I figured if Hillary trusted him, I could trust him," said Martin Waters, one of Mr. Hsu's investors (Dugan et al. 2007, A1). Norman Hsu visibly leveraged his dealings with Bill and Hillary Clinton to gain the trust of others, like Mr. Waters, so they might contribute money to his schemes. Mr. Hsu showed off a saxophone he owned, for example, which was autographed by President Clinton, and displayed a bomber jacket with the presidential seal to investor Waters, saying, "Bill Clinton gave this to me" (A14). At his New York City loft, Hsu displayed a collection of Hillary Clinton photos, videos, and personal thank-you letters from the ex-senator.

Like Lehman Brothers' security certificates and Big Man Ongka's pearl shells (see below), Norman Hsu's Clinton artifacts were displayed as visible tokens of trust. Seeing is believing, and the objects, though speechless themselves, spoke favorably on Mr. Hsu's behalf. As for the man's spoken idiom, Hsu often mumbled but he could speak passionately. His laughter, shy smile, and self-effacing mien lured others to his side on behalf of contributing money to elect more Democrats. As trust tokens, Hsu's saxophone and bomber jacket were visible enough. The only trouble was that they were ingenuine. Soon after joining Hillary's campaign fund-raising team, Hsu went to jail for stealing $60 million from investors in his bogus schemes (Dugan et al. 2007, A14).

IN PIGS WE TRUST

If trust matters for nebulous products like CDOs, it also matters for tangible goods like pork bellies. Pork-belly futures have been traded on the Chicago Mercantile Exchange since 1961. The unit of trade is a very solid twenty tons of frozen, trimmed pork bellies, from which U.S. bacon is made. Traders sign contractual agreements to buy or sell set numbers of pork-belly units at an agreed-upon future date. In effect, traders bet money on whether the price of bacon will rise or fall, and trust that all signatories will honor the contract.

In pork-belly trading, a visible token of trust is the contract itself, which is to say, the written certificate. Should one party renege, the matter would be settled in court. A judge or jury would consult the written document to ascertain violations of trust. But what if there were no such document? What if there were no written contracts, or indeed, no writing system whatsoever? Such is the case among pig traders in aboriginal New Guinea, where the visible tokens of trust are all nonverbal.

In the New Guinea Highlands, the case of the charismatic "Big Man" is an exotic example of what trust looks like in a world without writing. A Big Man (there are also "Big Women") is a tribal elder who leads through influence rather than authority. The Big Man neither dictates nor rules as a chief. Instead, he persuades.

New Guinea leadership comes about through visible displays of oratorical conviction and the eloquence of body language. For a Big Man, the most tangible tokens of trust are, respectively, the confidence displayed through his own bodily communication and the bodies of his own living pigs. In preliterate New Guinea, showing a healthy pig tethered to a wooden *olka* stake ritually driven into the ground is the aboriginal way of saying, "I show you the money." Pigs are trusted signs of wealth, and men without them are considered *etamb,* the Melpa word for "rubbish."

Big Men build extensive networks of trading partners with whom, at festive ceremonies called *mokas,* live pigs, cooked pig meat, and ornate pearl-shell heirlooms change hands. The most famous of all New Guinea Big Men is Ongka, the colorful and charismatic leader of the Kawelka tribe. Few men in the Highlands have the status or stature of Ongka.

In the classic documentary film *Ongka's Big Moka* (1974), the first thing you notice about the renowned Big Man is his confident stride. He walks with an energetic, muscular gait suggestive of certainty, self-assurance, and purpose. The way he walks with his head up, arms briskly swinging, and shoulders squared shows onlookers the man knows exactly where he is going, and why.

Ongka's rustic office near the Highlands town of Mount Hagen is within the ceremonial men's house. The round house is set in a cleared, grassy park bordered by flowers, pinelike casuarina trees, and leafy cordyline shrubs. Reminiscent of Bart McDade's superstition of parking his car in the same "magical" spot in order to keep financial markets rising, Kawelka men bury magical stones, cultivate magical ferns (*nong*), and plant red-flowering trees in their parkland to attract wealth. The verdant, campuslike setting is not unlike Microsoft's grassy office park in Redmond, Washington, where Michael Kinsley toiled in his modular workspace. Unlike Mr. Kinsley's workspace, however, inside Ongka's office you will find no telephone, e-mail, or keyboard—no written reports, text messages, or memos of any kind—and no printed contracts. In the Highlands of New Guinea, communication is strictly face-to-face and personal.

At a *moka* party near his office, Ongka dressed in bird-of-paradise feathers and a cordyline grass skirt—and wore a white pearl-shell pendant and green-snail earrings—to shout a speech to rival Big Men on the grounds. Even without a microphone Ongka's melodic tenor voice cut through the crowd. All within earshot clearly heard his pronouncements.

As he spoke, Ongka's body language showed an unimpeachable flair for leadership. As my colleague Kenneth Read wrote in his book *The High Valley*, Big Men typically give speeches "with sweeping, florid gestures punctuated with moments of studied immobility when a taut leg or outflung arm [lend] emphasis to words resting on the air like the sound of a vibrating string" (Read 1965, 20). Adding his own body's gravitas to spoken words, Ongka dramatically gestured and danced, kicked up his heels, marched back and forth in confident strides, brandished his steel axe, and ended his orations with drawn-out "o-o-o-o" sounds. Those who've seen *Ongka's Big Moka* will attest that his voice tones and body language are stunningly brilliant.

Ongka's career goal was to amass a fortune of six hundred pigs. But as the Kawelka tribe's premier Big Man, he would not keep even one animal for himself. Ongka would give each and every pig away. To assemble six hundred pigs in one place at one time requires major trust. Years before the *moka* was held, Ongka trusted that his network of far-flung trading partners would actually show up at the ceremony with all the pigs they owed. Trading partners, in turn, trusted that Ongka would give away all the pigs and not keep a single animal for himself.

Ongka's traditional work world is reminiscent of simpler times in the United States when deals were sealed not with wordy contracts but with simple binding handshakes. Yet if Ongka's tropical world is "simpler," it is also ceremonial, and far more exotic. Along with tethered pigs and theatrical body language, one of the paramount trust tokens is neither a handshake nor a document but a precious heirloom—an exquisitely mounted, luminous pearl shell. Among the Kawelka, two Torres Strait pearl shells (*Pinctada maxima*) are worth one small pig, and eight shells are worth one large pig. It is widely believed among the Kawelka that a pearl shell's gleam is a magical signal that attracts additional shells to a Big Man's side. This is the Kawelka version of Wall Street's cherished belief that "wealth attracts wealth."

Ongka's powerful body language and dramaturgy, his tethered pigs and those owed to him, and his impressive display of pearl shells earned Ongka unprecedented trust in the region. Capitalizing on the trust of Mount Hagen–area residents, in 1974 Ongka sponsored the biggest *moka* party ever given on Kawelka land. At the festive ceremony he gave away a record six hundred pigs and numerous other objects of value. Replete with visible tokens of trust, Ongka's big *moka* made him the most renowned elder of the Kawelka tribe. He won exceptional influence over, and indebtedness from, each of his rivals. In turn, each rival Big Man was expected to marshal his own tokens of trust, and eventually give back more than he'd received from Ongka. Since what was owed would be returned in a few short years with more than 100 percent interest, Ongka stood to become even wealthier. So great was the trust factor among his trading partners that the renowned Big Man would only get bigger still.

FROM PORK BELLY TO PONZI SCHEME

Unlike Ongka, who went barefoot, spoke Melpa, and lived in New Guinea, Bernard L. "Bernie" Madoff wore polished leather shoes, spoke English, and lived in Manhattan, New York. Also unlike Ongka, who presented a trustworthy image of himself on behalf of his *moka,* Madoff faked a trustworthy image to perpetrate an historic fraud. Ongka's face was open, sincere, and trustworthy in contrast to Madoff's, which had the pained look of trust disfigured.

As the Madoff scandal broke in December 2008, the first thing I noticed about the man was his tightly compressed lips. They were rolled in and pressed together so tightly I barely saw them. After studying the widely publicized photo by Don Emmert for Getty Images of Mr. Madoff's right-facial profile, my first impression of the man was that he had something serious to hide. The more I learned about him, the more I realized that Bernie Madoff's chronic lip inversion was symptomatic of something very serious, indeed. He had knowingly violated the trust of his investment clients—including the trust of his closest friend and mentor, Carl Shapiro (to the tune of $400 million)—and had bilked them out of an estimated $65 *billion.* That's a lot of pork bellies.

The man with the chronically disappearing lips had himself disappeared more money in his Ponzi scheme than had anyone else in the history of finance. Though he was clearly not a man to be trusted, many *did* trust Bernie Madoff to take care of their personal fortunes. What visible tokens of trust did his clients see? Why were so many so flabbergasted to learn—after Mr. Madoff confessed in December to his sons and the FBI—that their investments were null and void? Had no one read his lips?

As you learned in chapters I and 10, tense lips can signal negative emotions. In *The Nonverbal Dictionary* I define "tense-mouth" as (I) "a gesture produced by compressing, in-rolling, and narrowing the lips to a thin line," and (2) "a position of the mouth in which the lips are visibly tightened and pressed together through contraction of the lip and jaw muscles" (Givens 2009). Lips, the muscular, fleshy, hairless folds surrounding the mouth opening, are our most emotionally expressive body parts. Lip and jaw tension clearly reflects anxious feelings, nervousness, and emotional stress. An acutely tensed mouth can precisely mark the onset of a mood shift, a novel thought, or a sudden change of heart.

A tense-mouth expression may be chronic or acute. The lips of a chronically angry or upset person may "freeze" in a permanently tight-lipped expression, such as that shown in 1960s photographs of then–FBI director J. Edgar Hoover. In his later years the controversial Mr. Hoover was seen by many as a rigid, embittered, paranoid man. In contrast, an acute or temporary tense-mouth expression was captured in some photos of President Bill Clinton during his 1998 scandal, such as the well-publicized cover shot on the September 21, 1998, edition of *US News & World Report*. Earlier, as he sat in the Map Room of the White House on August 17, 1998, minutes before confessing to the American people—"Indeed, I did have a relationship with Ms. Lewinsky that was not appropriate"—Mr. Clinton's usually relaxed, everted lips compressed tightly, inverted, and disappeared from view.

More like Hoover's than Clinton's, Bernie Madoff's tense-mouth likely reflects a deeply troubled man, someone who has long felt the torment of disfigured trust. His once visible lips—seen in a 1960 photo of Mr. Madoff in happier times, serving as best man at a friend's wedding—vanished as the tense-mouth clamped down on his face. This facial expression is well studied. Monkeys and apes show compressed-lip expressions prior to attacking (Givens 1976). Children in threatening situations compress their lips (Stern and Bender 1974). Compressed lips are an aggressive sign in our nearest primate relative, the pygmy chimpanzee (Waal and Lanting 1997). In the Highlands of New Guinea, when tribal men were asked to show what they would do when angry and were about to attack, University of California psychologist Paul Ekman reported that "they pressed their lips together" (Ekman 1998, 238).

A gestural fossil left after millions of years of evolution, the tense-mouth display is innervated by special visceral nerves originally designed for feeding. The expression is emotionally responsive today and still reflects visceral sensations—gut feelings—aroused by aggression, anger, and fear. We tighten our lips to seal off the mouth opening in a form of "nonverbal lockdown" to protect the oral cavity from harmful chemicals, for example, or approaching enemies. Bernard Madoff's chronic tense-mouth is a likely response to the toxic financial world he created, a world that poisoned thousands of investors and brought revengeful clients to gather on the street below his high-rise penthouse door.

Prior to his Ponzi scheme's unraveling, Bernie had, like Ongka, worked for years to present a trustworthy image. His credentials were impeccable. He'd received a bachelor's degree from Hofstra University, spent a year at Brooklyn Law School, founded Bernard L. Madoff Investment Securities (BMIS), and chaired the NAS-DAQ stock exchange. He wore expensively tailored suits, collected

vintage timepieces, and lived in posh homes in the best neighbor-
hoods. He traveled in private jets, yachts, and expensive sedans.
Just as Ongka's New Guinea clansmen displayed pearl shells to
draw wealth from the countryside, Bernie Madoff displayed the
appurtenances of wealth to draw investors into his scheme. Never
given to the vocal hard sell, Mr. Madoff let his physical appearance and possessions do the talking.

BMIS was headquartered deep in the corporate canyons of New
York at 885 Third Avenue in a thirty-four-story office tower known
as the Lipstick Building. (The skyscraper is named for its oval shape
and red-enameled granite walls that resemble a giant tube of lipstick.) BMIS occupied the seventeenth, eighteenth, and nineteenth
floors. Bernard Madoff's personal office was on the seventeenth
floor. Through the years, however, Bernie spent a good deal of time
out of the office prospecting for clients on golf courses. Indeed, golf
courses were said to be his favorite hunting ground for new investors. He was a member of the Palm Beach Country Club and as
many as five other golfing clubs. Recall from chapter 12 that golfing
is the evolutionary correct way to build business rapport, and rapport Bernie built. According to finance author Peter Sander, "As
many as a third of Palm Beach Country Club's three hundred
members are said to be Madoff investors" (Sander 2009, 76).

If Madoff exploited through the evolutionary psychology of
golf, he also exploited by emitting visual and behavioral signs
of sameness. You may recall the reptilian principle of isopraxism
briefly sketched in chapter 10. Isopraxism—"same behavior"—is
the notion that by dressing alike, being members of the same country club, contributing to the same charities, and golfing together on
the same links, people feel subliminally bonded. Since "same is
safe," biologically, as in "birds of a feather," people may easily establish trust with others who are "just like them."

For a long time, Bernard Madoff, who is Jewish, preyed prin-
cipally on Jewish people who were "just like him." At country-club

affairs he wielded the same silver spoons, ate the same fancy meals off the same china plates, drank the same fine wine from identical stemware, and used the same linen napkins as others used to wipe his own hands and lips. The sameness that bonded him with golfing brethren culminated in "affinity fraud," the crime of stealing not from strangers but from people much like himself. By giving off their signature identity signals, he could easily take their cash. Before long, people were lining up—literally pleading, whining, and begging—to invest with the financial wizard, Bernie Madoff.

How could anybody have known the "someone like them" was a fraud? There were clues, but Bernard L. Madoff was so much like his victims that clues hardly mattered. A clear danger sign was that Madoff provided no background information or printed brochures on the funds in which he supposedly invested his clients' cash. Again unlike Ongka, whose rows of tethered pigs corporeally "showed you the money," Madoff showed nothing but bogus account statements on nonexistent investments. Client monies went directly to Chase Manhattan Bank and sat there, uninvested, until he withdrew funds for himself, or withdrew funds from newer "investors" to pay interest on older accounts (the classic Ponzi ploy). Since there were no securities investments at all, however, when clients wanted their money back as the economy fell in 2008, there was none to give them. There were simply no pigs left in Mr. Madoff's poke.

Another danger sign was Bernie Madoff's conspicuous need for secrecy. Unlike Ongka, for whom everything from his bird-of-paradise feathers to his self-assured stride was on public display, much of Bernie's daily business life was hidden. While the eighteenth and nineteenth floors of the Lipstick Building were filled with Madoff files and busy employees, the entire seventeenth level—Bernie's floor—was staffed with only twenty or so rather mysterious colleagues. Few from the higher levels or the outside world ever visited the seventeenth floor, which has been characterized as Bernie Madoff's "sanctum."

Hidden from View

"Why the need for such secrecy?" Harry Markopolos asked about Bernard L. Madoff (Sander 2009, 100). In 2000 Boston-based Rampart Investment Management Company tasked employee Markopolos with researching Madoff's investment strategy to see if Rampart could match Mr. Madoff's consistently high returns on investments. Unable to replicate the strategy, Mr. Markopolos surmised that Bernie Madoff could be running a Ponzi scheme.

One of Harry Markopolos's key suspicions about a possible Ponzi scheme had to do with Madoff's secrecy. Secrecy was a sign that Bernie Madoff may have been using illegal means to profit from his too-trusting investors.

The English word "secrecy" is the quality or condition of being secret, hidden, or concealed (Soukhanov 1992, 1630). The English word derives from the seven-thousand-year-old Indo-European word *krei-*, "secret." Throughout *Your Body at Work* I've traced important words like "rapport," "sight," and "trust" to their ancient roots to learn where the words come from, how they evolved, and what hidden connotations they might hold today.

Victims of Bernard Madoff's Ponzi scheme may be interested to learn that important derivatives of the Indo-European root word *krei-* include "riddle," "garble," "criminal," "crisis," "hypocrisy," and "excrement," a fitting tribute to the tight-lipped wizard of finance.

One of the more cryptic colleagues on the seventeenth floor was Frank DiPascali, who'd been with Mr. Madoff for more than thirty years. "A high school graduate with a Queens accent," *Fortune* magazine reported, "he came to work in an incongruously starched version of a slacker's uniform: pressed jeans, a sweatshirt, and pristine white sneakers or boat shoes. He could often be found outside the building, smoking a cigarette" (Bandler et al. 2009).

"Nobody was quite sure what he did or what his title was," the article went on. "'He was like a ninja,' says a former trader in the legitimate operation upstairs [on the nineteenth floor]. 'Everyone knew he was a big deal, but he was like a shadow'" (Bandler et al. 2009). Mr. DiPascali was often the only Madoff employee in Bernie's office when deals were made between Madoff and the partners who provided "feeder" funds for the illicit Ponzi scheme.

Researchers have commented on the problem of finding public information about the elusive Bernard Madoff. "A look at the 1960 Hofstra University yearbook should bring some information to light about Mr. Madoff," Peter Sander writes, "yet it does not. Apparently he wasn't mentioned, nor did he appear in any photos, in that yearbook. Classmates interviewed did not remember him, either" (Sander 2009, 25). Secrecy, it seems, became him from the very beginning of his career.

Bernie rarely met even with his own clients. "While he managed billions of dollars for individuals and foundations," *The New York Times* reported, "he shunned one-on-one meetings with most of his investors, wrapping himself in an Oz-like aura, making him even more desirable to those seeking access" (Creswell and Thomas 2009). Like the Wizard of Oz, Bernard L. Madoff, built trust through illusion. As the aphorism at the beginning of this chapter reads, "It takes years to build up trust, and only seconds to destroy it."

In the business world, trust is most often viewed as an intangible. Intangibles such as goodwill and teamwork are incapable of being perceived by the senses, or of being realized or defined (Soukhanov 1992, 937). As you have seen in this chapter, however, trust also has a tangible, corporeal side shown in visible tokens of conduct or misconduct. Bart McDade's parking place, Richard Fuld's CDO certificates, Ongka's pigs and pearl shells, and Bernard Madoff's chronic tense-mouth are all available to the senses as visible tokens of trust—or mistrust.

Visible trust signs are almost always available in the workplace, but to be useful they must be read. Recall that sight-reading is the act of anticipating intentions and moods through the perceptive examination of nonverbal cues. Sight-reading is an active process, one that requires mental dedication and constant practice. Since you've nearly finished reading *Your Body at Work,* I believe you are well on your way.

In the concluding chapter, you will visit a workplace known for its complete absence of privacy. Within its walls, every movement of every body is watched. It's a step toward a likely future world wherein every footstep, keystroke, and body movement in the workplace will be monitored.

Conclusion:
Your Body at Work

**When people come to me with business propositions,
I use tells to determine if these individuals
feel their proposition is "strong" or "weak,"
whether it is reasonable or exaggerated.**

—Phil Hellmuth, Jr., winner of eleven World Series of Poker bracelets

Recall poker expert Joe Navarro's comment about body language in chapter 1: "The major purpose of observation at the poker table is intelligence gathering—you want to learn as much as you can about each of your opponents at the table" (Navarro 2006, 10–11). I commented that whether you're seated at a card table or a conference table, the stakes are high, and watching body language will give you an advantage in the game. Like tells at the poker table, body movements tip hands at the board table as well.

Though not a gambler myself, I was delighted to speak as a keynoter at Caesars Palace in Las Vegas, Nevada, at the fourth annual World Game Protection Conference in 2009. My talk on "Crime Signals in Casinos" summarized observations I'd made in Atlantic City, Las Vegas, and Spokane-area casinos. With the lure of food and drink, entertainment, and easy money, the casino habitat brings in people from all walks of life. There's no better place to watch body language than at a baccarat, blackjack, or craps table.

At Caesars Palace, sight-reading—the perceptive examination of nonverbal cues—is more than just observation. Sight-reading at Caesars is a full-time occupation. Security personnel there are paid to watch casino patrons and staff, and each other, twenty-four hours a day. Since the produce of gaming tables is chips and cash, and since human beings are primates with clever, grasping hands, casinos face the perennial problem of theft. Security workers cope with late bets, card switching, chip filching, paying of losing hands, and dealer-patron collusion, and they do so through continuous examination of body-language signs.

In a casino sight-reading is constant and consistent, never casual. Closed-circuit television (CCTV) cameras monitor behavior throughout the casino grounds, from restaurants and bars to cashier cages and card rooms. High-resolution "eye in the sky" cameras above gaming areas—colloquially known as the Eye—enable surveillance agents to see suspicious body language, abnormal actions, hands where they shouldn't be, and bodies out of place.

Cheating at a craps table, for example, often involves a distraction such as stirring up a ruckus or causing a disturbance to take dealers' eyes off the dice. Since distraction methods are usually exaggerated, they're easily picked up by the Eye in the sky. Specially trained surveillance agents also decode subtle chip-stacking signals that poker-collusion-team players use to tell each other what cards they hold in their hands. Indeed, in few other workplaces is sight-reading as intensive, effective, or high-tech as it is in a modern casino.

With diligent practice in observation, and by applying what you've learned in *Your Body at Work,* your own workplace can be as readable as any in the gaming industry. In fact, you have an advantage. Since you see co-workers on an hourly, daily, and weekly basis, you know whom you're dealing with. Unlike the casino's facial-recognition software, used to spot criminals and recidivist cheats, all you need to decode your workplace is a bold and fearless eye. The more you watch people's bodies as you listen to their words, the better you'll become in every facet of your job. So keep your personnel manual in the desk drawer where it belongs—and open your eyes to the body at work. May you enjoy the sensory drama of your workplace as never before.

Bibliography

Adamy, Janet. 2007. "Starbucks Chairman Says Trouble May Be Brewing." *The Wall Street Journal* (http://www.online.wsj.com, February 24, accessed February 25, 2007).

Adena. (a) 2001. Personal communication, April 10, 2001.

Adena. (b) 2001. Personal communication, April 12, 2001.

Agins, Teri. 2008. "Women Fall Head Over Heels for Shoe Makers' Arch Designs." *The Wall Street Journal*, October 14.

Alford, Richard. 1996. "Adornment." In *Encyclopedia of Cultural Anthropology*, ed. David Levinson and Melvin Ember, pp. 7–9 New York: Henry Holt.

Alston, Jon P., and Isao Takei. 2005. *Japanese Business Culture and Practices*. New York: iUniverse.

Altmann, Stuart. 1967. "The Structure of Primate Communication." In *Social Communication Among Primates*, ed. Stuart Altmann, pp. 325–62. Chicago: University of Chicago Press.

Andrea. 2006. Personal Weblog, October 27, 2006. http://alphabetgame.blogspot.com/2006_10_01_archive.html (accessed August 8, 2008).

Andrews, Helena. 2008. "Was Hillary Faking?" Politico.com (http://www.politico.com, January 9, 2008, accessed January 9, 2008).

Anonymous. 1998. "Civility Pays Dividends." *San Diego Union-Tribune* (July 6), p. C1.

Anonymous. 2005. "Pope, Donald Trump's Hair Among Top Costume Picks." WSBTV Web site, October 31: http://www.wsbtv.com/halloween/5213331/detail.html. (accessed September 22, 2008).

Anonymous. (a) 2007. Comments posted to the *Times Educational Supplement* Web site, March 21, 2007. http://www.tes.co.uk. (accessed June 24, 2008).

Anonymous. (b) 2007. Comments posted to the Toxic Boss Web site, April 11, 2007. http://www.toxicboss.com/stories/index.html. (accessed June 15, 2008).

Anonymous. (c) 2007. "Cost of Edwards' Haircut Hits $1,250." *CBS News*, July 5, 2007. http://www.cbsnews.com (accessed November 10, 2008).

Anonymous. (d) 2007. "James Cayne Lashes Back at *WSJ* Report." *CNNMoney.com*, November 1, 2007. http://money.cnn.com (accessed August 5, 2008).

Anonymous. (a) 2008. "Witness: Office Shooting Suspect Was Polite." April 22, 2008. http://www.clickondetroit.com (accessed August 6, 2008).

Anonymous. (b) 2008. "Toxic Bosses: How to Live with the S.O.B." *BusinessWeek*, August 14, 2008. http://www.businessweek.com (accessed May 28, 2009).

Anonymous. (c) 2008. Happy Office Assistant (job announcement), November, 24, 2008. http://newyork.craigslist.org (accessed December 11, 2008).

Anonymous. 2009. "Do You Have a Copy of That?" *InfoWorld*, May 4, 2009. http://www.infoworld.com (accessed May 15, 2009).

Auletta, Ken. 1996. "The Re-education of Michael Kinsley." *The New Yorker*, May 13, 1996. http://www.kenauletta.com (accessed August 23, 2008).

Bacon, James A. 2007. "Building 14." Q&A interview with Mark Golan, Cisco Systems, February 5. http://www.baconsrebellion.com (accessed September 27, 2008).

Baile, Jeff. (a) 2000. "'Bowing Out' Means Trouble." *International Game Warden* (Fall), pp. 8–9.

Baile, Jeff. (b) 2000. Personal communication, July 29, 2000.

Ballmer, Steve. 1999. "Steve Ballmer Speech Transcript—'Developing Web Applications' Press Briefing." Press release, September 13, 1999. http://www.microsoft.com (accessed May 26, 2009).

Bandler, James, Nicholas Varchaver, and Doris Burke. 2009. "How Bernie Madoff Did It." cnnmoney.com, April 24, 2009. http://money.cnn.com (accessed June 22, 2009).

Beck, Melinda. 2008. "Hair Apparent? New Science on the Genetics of Balding." *The Wall Street Journal*, October 14.

Bennett, Julie. 2001. "A Heavy Burden." *Spokesman-Review*, April 22.

Bing, Stanley. 2004. "There Is No Crying in Business." *Fortune*, October 18, 2004. http://money.cnn.com (accessed August 5, 2008).

Binkley, Christina. 2007. "Wall Street Women: Dress Code of Silence." *The Wall Street Journal*, March 22.

———. (a) 2008. "How to Pull Off 'CEO Casual.'" *The Wall Street Journal*, August 7, 2008.

———. (b) 2008. "The Suit That Turns Me into a VIP." *The Wall Street Journal*, October 30.

Bixler, Susan. 1984. *The Professional Image*. New York: G. P. Putnam's Sons.

Brannigan, Christopher, and David Humphries. 1972. "Human Non-Verbal Behaviour, A Means of Communication." In *Ethological Studies of Child Behaviour*, ed. N. G. Blurton-Jones, pp. 37–64. Cambridge: University Press.

Brooks, Andrée Aelion. 2008. "Shoes 'R' Us." *The Wall Street Journal*, October 18–19.

Burgoon, Judee K., David B. Buller, and W. Gill Woodall. 1989. *Nonverbal Communication: The Unspoken Dialogue*. New York: Harper & Row.

Burns, Judith. 2007. "Sell Signal: When Boss Buys Trophy Home." *The Wall Street Journal*, April 12.

Burrough, Bryan, and John Helyar. 1990. *Barbarians at the Gate: The Fall of RJR Nabisco*. New York: Harper & Row.

Byrnes, Nanette. 2006. "Making the Job Meaningful All the Way Down the Line." *BusinessWeek*, May 1.

Capuzzo, Mike. 1991. "The Tiger Tamer, Out of the Spotlight." *Washington Post*, July 6, pp. C1, C8.

Casey, Nicholas. 2008. "Bratz Dolls Begin to Show Their Age." *The Wall Street Journal*, September 22.

Chan, James. 2009. "18 Practical Tips on Working with Your Chinese Partners." http://www.asiamarketingmanagement.com (accessed May 9, 2009).

Chesbro, George C. 1977. *Shadow of a Broken Man*. New York: Simon & Schuster.

Clark, Andrew. 2006. "Gates Cuts Back on Microsoft Role to Concentrate on Charity Projects." *The Guardian*, June 16, 2006. http://www.guardian.co.uk (accessed May 26, 2009).

Collett, P. 1983. "Mossi Salutations." *Semiotica* 45:191–248.

Collier, Lorna. 2004. "When a Good Cry Just Doesn't Work." October 6, 2004. http://www.lornacollier.com (accessed August 5, 2008).

Covel, Simona. 2008. "Wine Enthusiast Aims for Wider Audience." *The Wall Street Journal*, October 6. http://www.smsmallbiz.com (accessed October 6, 2008).

Craig, Susanne. (a) 2008. "Lehman Vet Grapples With the Firm's Repair." *The Wall Street Journal*, September 4.

———. (b) 2008. "Lawmakers Lay into Lehman CEO." *The Wall Street Journal*, October 7.

Creswell, Julie, and Landon Thomas, Jr. 2009. "The Talented Mr. Madoff." *The New York Times*, January 24, 2009. http://www.nytimes.com (accessed May 30, 2009).

Cruver, Brian. 2002. *Anatomy of Greed: The Unshredded Truth from an Enron Insider*. New York: Carroll & Graf.

Darwin, Charles. 1872. *The Expression of the Emotions in Man and Animals*. 3rd ed. New York: Oxford University Press, 1998.

Dugan, Ianthe Jeanne, Emshwiller, John R., Cheng, Jonathan, and Jim Carlton. 2007. "How a Business Flop Became Political Force." *The Wall Street Journal*, November 12.

Eichenwald, Kurt. 2005. *Conspiracy of Fools: A True Story*. New York: Broadway Books.

Ekman, Paul. 1998. Commentaries on *The Expression of the Emotions in Man and Animals*, by Charles Darwin (1872). 3rd ed. New York: Oxford University Press, 1998.

Fowler, James H. and Nicholas A. Christakis. 2008. "Dynamic Spread of Happinesss in a Large Social Network: Longitudinal Analysis Over 20 Years in the Framingham Heart Study," December 4, 2008, *British Medical Journal* (Vol. 337, pp. 2338). December 4. http://www.bmj.com (accessed December 6, 2008).

Garcia, Joaquin. 2008. *Making Jack Falcone: An Undercover FBI Agent Takes Down a Mafia Family*. New York: Touchstone.

Givens, David B. 1976. An Ethological Approach to the Study of Human Nonverbal Communication. Ph.D. dissertation in anthropology, University of Washington.

———. 1986. "The Big and the Small: Toward a Paleontology of Gesture." *Sign Language Studies*, no. 51:145–67.

———. 2005. *Love Signals: A Practical Field Guide to the Body Language of Courtship*. New York: St. Martin's Press.

———. 2009. *The Nonverbal Dictionary of Gestures, Signs, and Body Language Cues*. The Center for Nonverbal Studies. http://www.center-for-nonverbal-studies.org.

Gladwell, Malcolm. 2005. *Blink: The Power of Thinking Without Thinking*. New York: Little, Brown and Company.

Goldin-Meadow, Susan. 2005. *Hearing Gestures: How Our Hands Help Us Think*. Cambridge, Massachusetts: Harvard University Press.

Gur, Raquel E. 1975. "Conjugate Lateral Eye Movements as an Index of Hemispheric Activation." *Journal of Personality and Social Psychology* 31:751–57.

Gutner, Toddi. 2008. "Applicants' Personalities Put to the Test." *The Wall Street Journal*, August 26.

Hagan, Joe. 2008. "Only the Men Survive: The Crash of Zoe Cruz." *New York*, April 27, 2008. http://nymag.com (accessed October 19, 2008).

Hall, Edward T. 1959. *The Silent Language*. Garden City, New York: Doubleday.

Hall, Karl, and Irven DeVore. 1972. "Baboon Social Behavior." In *Primate Patterns*, ed. Phyllis Dolhinow, pp. 125–80. San Francisco: Holt, Rinehart, and Winston.

Harnad, Stevan. 1972. "Creativity, Lateral Saccades and the Nondominant Hemisphere." *Perceptual and Motor Skills* 34:653–54.

Heckscher, Melissa. 2008. "Shoe Reading: Donna Sozio Proves That Shoe Size Does Matter." LA.com, March 3, 2008. http://www.la.com (accessed May 26, 2009).

Honan, William H. 2001. "H. R. Ball, 79, Ad Executive Credited With Smiley Face." *The New York Times*, April 14.

Jargon, Julie. 2008. "Neatness Counts at Kyocera and at Others in the 5S Club." *The Wall Street Journal*, October 27.

Jen. 2006. "Getting Undressed." Personal Weblog, June 17, 2006. http://www.jenandtonic.ca/2006/06/getting_undressed.php (accessed May 2, 2008).

Jones, Joy. 1992. "Meaningful Steps." *The Washington Post*, September 11, p. D5.

Kanfer, F. 1960. "Verbal Rate, Eyeblink, and Content in Structured Psychiatric Interviews." *Journal of Abnormal and Social Psychology* (Vol. 61, No. 3), pp. 341–47.

Karson, Craig N. 1992. "Oculomotor Disorders in Schizophrenia." Ch. 56, pp. 414–421 in Anthony B. Joseph and Robert R. Young (eds.), *Movement Disorders in Neurology and Neuropsychiatry*, Blackwell Scientific Pubs., Inc., Cambridge, Mass.

Keddie, Andrew. 2009. "A Fine Slice of Bakewell's Art." The Southern Reporter, May 14, 2009. www.thesouthernreporter.co.uk (accessed May 15, 2009).

Kresse, Jim (compiler). 2001. "Casual Dress at Work Falls Victim to Slowdown." *Spokesman-Review*, July 29.

LaFrance, Marianne. 2000. "An Experimental Investigation into the Effects of 'Bad Hair.'" Study financed by Procter & Gamble's Physique (January).

Laskas, Jeanne Marie. 1988. "The Pet Shrink." *Washington Post Magazine*, November 20, pp. 34–39.

Lawick-Goodall, Jane van. 1968. "The Behaviour of Free-Living Chimpanzees in the Gombe Stream Reserve." *Behavioural Monographs* 1:161–311.

LeDoux, Joseph. 1995. "Emotion: Clues from the Brain." *Annual Review of Psychology* 46:209–35.

———. 1996. *The Emotional Brain: The Mysterious Underpinnings of Emotional Life.* New York: Simon & Schuster.

Lehman Brothers. 2007. 2007 Annual Report. http://www.fliiby.com, n.d. (accessed January 5, 2008).

Leow, Jason. 2007. "Chinese Bigwigs Are Quick to Reach For the Hair Color." *The Wall Street Journal*, December 11.

Lieberman, Philip. 1991. *Uniquely Human: The Evolution of Speech, Thought, and Selfless Behavior.* Cambridge: Harvard University Press.

MacLean, Paul D. 1990. *The Triune Brain in Evolution.* New York: Plenum Press.

Manthey, Toby. 2008. "Tests Tag Workers' Good, Bad Traits." *Arkansas Democrat Gazette*, October 26, 2008. http://www.nwanews.com (accessed December 3, 2008).

Mattioli, Dana. 2008. "Layoff Sign: Boss's Cold Shoulder." *The Wall Street Journal*, October 23.

Mazur, Allan, and C. Keating. 1984. "Military Rank Attainment of a West Point Class: Effects of Cadets' Physical Features." *American Journal of Sociology* 90:125–50.

McCracken, Grant. 1996. *Big Hair: A Journey into the Transformation of Self.* Woodstock, New York: The Overlook Press.

Megan. 2001. Personal communication, April 10.

Melnick, Arnold. 2007. "Let's Improve Our Office Demeanor." *The DO* (newsletter of the American Osteopathic Association), September, p. 14.

Miller, Ben. 2005. "Business Golf has Little to do with Putting." *Puget Sound Business Journal*, April 15, 2005. http://www.bizjournals.com/seattle (accessed August 5, 2007).

Milton, Pat. 2007. "Behavioural Analysis Helps Catch Spies, Poker Tells." *Globe and Mail*, October 22, 2007. http://www.globeandmail.com.

Miodownik, Mark. 2008. "Strands of Darwin's Hair are a Fitting Display: Our Hair's Story Is Entwined with That of Evolution." *The Guardian*, November 17, 2008. http://www.guardian.co.uk (accessed November 20, 2008).

Morris, Desmond. 1994. *Bodytalk: The Meaning of Human Gestures.* New York: Crown Publishers.

National Business Review (NBR). 2005. "Ad Exec Grabs Best Dressed Headlines." NBR Press release published on www.scoop.co.nz, October 15. (accessed January 10, 2009).

Navarro, Joseph. 2001. Personal communication, August 7.

———. 2006. *Read 'Em and Reap.* New York: HarperCollins.

Needleman, Sarah. 2008. "Snack Vendor—or Undercover Job Recruiter." *The Wall Street Journal*, September 9. http://www.online.wsj.com (accessed September 9, 2008).

Newstead, Adrian. 2002. "Guboo, Man With a Dream." *Sydney Morning Herald*, June 8. http://www.smh.com.au. (accessed January 5, 2008).

Nishiyama, Kazuo. 2000. *Doing Business with Japan: Successful Strategies for Intercultural Communication*. Honolulu: University of Hawaii Press.

Nooyi, Indra. 2005. "Indra Nooyi's Graduation Remarks." *BusinessWeek*, May 20, 2005. http://www.businessweek.com (accessed October 13, 2008).

O'Brien, Timothy L. 2005. *Trump Nation: The Art of Being the Donald*. New York: Warner Business Books.

Oldenburg, Ann. 2004. "Fire the Signature Comb-over, Stylists Say." *USA Today*, January 20, 2004. http://www.usatoday.com.

O'Neill, Samantha. 2008. "Feathers: A Flight of Fancy." My Fashion Life, December 1, 2008. http://www.myfashionlife .com (accessed December 2, 2008).

Orwall, Bruce. 2004. "In Court Case, a Vivid Portrayal of Eisner's Boardroom Tactics." *The Wall Street Journal*, November 23.

Peek, Liz. 2008. "Goldman Sachs Before the Storm." *The Wall Street Journal*, October 1.

Plumb, Christian, and Dan Wilchins. 2008. "Lehman CEO Fuld's Hubris Contributed to Meltdown." Reuters, September 14, 2008. http://www.reuters.com (accessed November 5, 2008).

Que, Kappa. 2008. Web comment, October 21, 2008. http:// www.brotherhoodofbaldpeople.com (accessed October 28, 2008).

Read, Kenneth E. 1965. *The High Valley*. New York: Charles Scribner's Sons.

Richter, Stephan. 2008. "Milling Around at Starbucks: An Open Letter to Howard Schultz." *The Globalist*, June 20, 2008. http://www.theglobalist.com (accessed December 12, 2008).

Rockefeller, David. 2002. *Memoirs*. New York: Random House.

S., Alex. 2007. Web comment, December 7, 2007. http://www.yelp. com (accessed December 12, 2008).

S., Millard. 2008. Web comment, March 31, 2008. http://www. bnet.com (accessed December 12, 2008).

Sander, Peter. 2009. *Madoff: Corruption, Deceit, and the Making of the World's Most Notorious Ponzi Scheme.* Guilford, Connecticut: Globe Pequot Press.

Sapir, Edward. 1929. "The Unconscious Patterning of Behavior in Society." In *The Unconscious: A Symposium*, ed. E.S. Dummer, pp. 114–42. New York: Knopf.

Scott, Sophfronia. 2000. "The Big Bang." *People Weekly*, November 27, p. 129.

Shellenbarger, Sue. 2008. "When Tough Times Weigh on the Kids." *The Wall Street Journal*, September 24.

Showalter, Elaine. 2001. "Fade to Greige." *London Review of Books* 23, no. 1, (January 14). http://www.lrb.co.uk (accessed February 2007).

Simonidou, Athina. 2007. "Photo Galleries: Katie Couric." http:// www.tunc.biz/couric_fan.htm. (accessed March 27).

Smith, Randall, Anita Raghavan, and Ann Davis. 2007. "How Zoe Cruz Lost Her Job on Wall Street." *The Wall Street Journal*, December 1–2.

Smith, Ray. 2008. "An Ironic Look for Lean Times: Extreme Banker." *The Wall Street Journal*, October 23.

Sommer, Robert. 1967. "Small Group Ecology." *Psychological Bulletin* 67, no. 2:145–52.

Soukhanov, Anne H., ed. 1992. *The American Heritage Dictionary of the English Language.* New York: Houghton Mifflin.

———. 1993. "Word Watch." *The Atlantic Monthly*, October, p. 135.

Spinney, Laura. 2000. "Bodytalk." *New Scientist*, April 8.

Spors, Kelly K. 2008. "Top Small Workplaces 2008." *The Wall Street Journal*, October 13.

Stein, Bob. 2008. "Study Says Happiness Spreads Like Virus." *The Washington Post*, December 5.

Stein, Sarah. 2008. *Plumes*. New Haven, Conn.: Yale University Press.

Stern, Daniel and Estelle Bender. 1974. "An Ethological Study of Children Approaching a Strange Adult." In *Sex Differences in Behavior*, eds. Richard Friedman et al, pp. 233–58. New York: John Wiley and Sons.

Strathern, Andrew. 1979. *Ongka: A Self-Account by a New Guinea Big-Man*. New York: St. Martin's Press.

Tabuchi, Hiroko. 2008. "Building Beard Buzz." *The Wall Street Journal*, June 24.

Tierney, John. 2000. "Can Power Transcend Knotted Silk?" *The New York Times*, December 1, 2000. http://www.nytimes.com (accessed July 12, 2009).

Tong, Vinnee. 2008. "CEO Richard Fuld to Leave Lehman by Year-End." Associated Press, November 6, 2008. http://ap.google.com (accessed November 7, 2008).

Trueheart, Charles. 1995. "The Right Scuff: Toronto's Shoe Museum." *The Washington Post*, May 17.

Tuna, Cari, and Keith J. Winstein. 2008. "Economy Promises to Fuel Résumé Fraud." *The Wall Street Journal*, November 17, 2008. http://online.wsj.com (accessed November 19, 2008).

Vienne, Véronique. 1997. "Reinventing the Rules." *Style* magazine, September 1997, pp. 149–52, 154, 156, 158, 160.

Virginia, 2007. Anonymous review of Brunomagli's "Jolyn" shoe, March 9. http://www.zappos.com (accessed March 23, 2007).

Vrij, Aldert, Lucy Akehurst, and Paul Morris. 1997. "Individual Differences in Hand Movements During Deception." *Journal of Nonverbal Behavior* 21, no. 2:87–102.

Waal, Frans de, and Frans Lanting. 1997. *Bonobo: The Forgotten Ape*. Berkeley: University of California Press.

Welch, Jack, and Suzy Welch. 2008. "Release Your Inner Extrovert." *BusinessWeek*, December 8.

White, Gregory L. 2008. "The Bitter Battle to Lead TNK-BP." *The Wall Street Journal*, July 23. http://www.online.wsj.com (accessed July 30, 2008).

White, Renee. 2002. "Hands Speak a Thousand Words." *Amsterdam News*, September 4, 2002. http://www.amsterdamnews.com (accessed November 2007).

Winstein, Keith J. 2008. "Inflated Credentials Surface in Executive Suite." *The Wall Street Journal*, November 13.

Woo, Elaine. 2001. "Designer of 'Smiley Face' Dies at Age 79." *Spokesman-Review*. (*Los Angeles Times* story, April 15).

The Body Can Give Us Many Clues....

"By knowing what signs to look for (and what signs to put out) you can find the dating process a much more agreeable experience."
—*The Sacramento Bee*

"This book is not just for law enforcement officers, it is for anyone who is concerned about their own safety and the safety of their loved ones. This is a must read."
—Joe Navarro, FBI Special Agent (Ret.), author of *What Every Body Is Saying*